Which Way to Happiness?

Is there a way to find *real* happiness?
Yes!
There is a **real** way that is both unique and radical.
It came from Jesus.
Which Way to Happiness? shares Jesus' prescription for contemporary Christians of every generation. If we take His radical message of truths from the Beatitudes seriously, we will never be the same. He is the only way to *real* happiness!

Which Way to Happiness?

A Bible Commentary for Laymen/The Beatitudes
BY DAN BAUMANN

Regal
Books

A Division of GL Publications
Ventura, CA U.S.A.

Other good reading in this series:
Highlights of the Bible/Genesis to
    Nehemiah by Ray C. Stedman
Highlights of the Bible/New Testament by
    William L. Lane
Parables of Luke by D. Stuart Briscoe

The foreign language publishing of all Regal books is under the direction of GLINT. GLINT provides financial and technical help for the adaptation, translation and publishing of books for millions of people worldwide. For information regarding translation, contact: GLINT, P.O. Box 6688, Ventura, California 93006.

Third Printing, 1982

Published by Regal Books
A Division of GL Publications
Ventura, California 93006

Library of Congress Catalog Card No. 81-50302
ISBN 0-8307-0773-5

Editor's note: For the sake of easier reading, the use of *he, him* and *his* in this publication refers for the most part to both male and female in the generic sense.

CONTENTS

A Teacher's Manual and Student Discovery Guides for Bible study groups using this book are available from your church supplier.

CHAPTER ONE

Christian Counterculture

Matthew 5:1,2

I was 45 years old when I received my first speeding ticket. Now for someone who is on the road as much as I am—I traveled 10,000 miles this past summer visiting churches—that may not be too bad a record. I started driving when I was 14 years old. We lived in Wisconsin at the time and I got a farm permit which allowed me to drive at the age of 14. So I feel that I have driven long enough and far enough that I am quite competent. Ordinarily I drive the way I should. I live righteously on the roads.

But this particular day I was out with my kids. We went to Lake Delores to spend the day on the big water slides. If you have been there you know that Lake Delores is right out in the middle of nothing—no heavy traffic, just a lot of open country. I was driving along, talking to my kids, when I saw this light flashing behind me. I pulled over, stopped, handed over my driver's license, pleaded my case, and almost cried. The officer kept right on writing out my ticket. I called the police station in Victorville and asked them, "What am I going to do? I've never had a speeding ticket before. I don't want this on my record. I don't want anyone to know about this."

The person on the other end of the line replied, "Go to traffic school." So on Tuesday and Thursday nights, from 6:00 to 10:00 I sat in traffic school—with about 45 other criminals in society—in those little student chairs with the wrap-around armrest on which you take notes. I have a full-cut body and I thought they were going to have to hacksaw me out of the seat by the end of the first two hours.

At that first class the instructor said some things that impressed me.

Among them was this statement: "Usually the folks in my classes are not bad drivers. Most of you are young." (There were only five of us over 20 years of age.) "Just haven't had enough experience, just made a mistake. Some of you just kind of got used to driving and became careless." That's what really happened with me. I was going 65 miles on the open highway in the 55-mile-an-hour zone. I just sat back on my good driving record. I quit sharpening my skill, or improving my abilities as a driver.

This statement was reinforced before the evening

was over. At the end of the first two-hour session we were given a 20-minute break. The instructor warned us in advance that he would not start the class until everyone was back in his seat. At the end of the break we filed back into the class; four members were missing. Finally, after we had waited a while, they walked in looking very sheepish. The instructor gently rebuked them and asked, "Why are you so late?" The spokesman for the group said, "I'm sorry. We went out for a Coke and on the way back we had an auto accident."

"Some of you just kind of got used to driving." I believe this is what has happened to the church today. We have become so accustomed to "church" that it has lost its cutting edge. Rather than being a force in the midst of the world, the church has become just a part of the flow of things; it simply moves along without a piercing message that makes it distinctive. As a result the church has become lost in the rest of our culture, without steel, without challenge.

As we look at the Beatitudes I want you to see that they were given to us by Jesus so that our lives would be challenged and we would change. Jesus' Sermon on the Mount, Matthew 5, 6, and 7, confronts us with a message that calls us to a distinctiveness of life, a commitment that is unique and, in the midst of the church and in the midst of the world, is a message of clarity and conviction in its distinctiveness. John Stott has written a book on the Sermon on the Mount entitled *Christian Counter-Culture*. By this he is saying that we as Christians are not supposed to just follow culture; we are supposed to stand up and be, in the midst of our culture, a distinctive, quality people. Throughout this book we are going to look at the Beatitudes and ask the Spirit of God to minister to us so that we become that "counter-culture"—distinctive, qualitatively unique; God's own chosen people.

Introduction to Matthew

The author of the book of Matthew is Matthew himself. Luke, in his Gospel, tells us more about him than Matthew tells about himself. Luke says: "And after that He [Jesus] went out, and noticed a tax-gatherer named Levi [Matthew], sitting in the tax office, and He said to him, 'Follow me.' And he left everything behind, and rose up and began to follow Him. And Levi gave a big reception for Him in his house; and there was a great crowd of tax-gatherers and other people who were re-clining at table with them" (Luke 5:27-29).

Matthew says of his calling, "And as Jesus passed on from there, He saw a man, called Matthew, sitting in the tax office; and He said to him, 'Follow Me!' And he rose and followed Him" (Matt 9:9). These two passages tell us three things about Matthew: (1) his father named him Levi; (2) he was a tax collector; (3) he became a disciple of Jesus.

The name Levi relates to the priestly order. It is very possible that Matthew's father, being a godly man, named his son Levi and prayed with expectation that

God would take his boy and make him a power for God. But something happened in his son's life and the boy began running around with the crooks of the day. He became part of the culture that was looked down on by thoughtful people. Even Jesus didn't have much good to say about tax collectors: "For if you love those who love you, what reward have you? Do not even the tax gatherers do the same?" (Matt. 5:46). "Truly I say to you that the tax-gatherers and harlots will get into the kingdom of God before you [scribes and chief priests]" (Matt. 21:31). The name "tax-gatherer" was synonymous with sinners: "And it happened that as He [Jesus] was reclining at table in the house, behold many tax-gatherers and sinners came and joined Jesus and His disciples at the table. And when the Pharisees saw this, they said to His disciples, 'Why does your Teacher eat with the tax-gatherers and sinners?' " (Matt. 9:10,11).

A tax collector in the first century was a man committed to graft and dishonesty. It was part of the job. So Matthew was not the Levi his father had hoped he would be. It is kind of like naming a son John—"a man sent from God"—and having him join the Mafia.

But one day Matthew met Jesus and his life took a U-turn. Undoubtedly, Matthew was the most educated of the Twelve, a gifted writer, a man who, according to some traditions, was slain by the sword—martyred. Although Mark's Gospel was the first written, Matthew's was chosen to be the first book in the New Testament. Mark's Gospel was the historical foundation which both Matthew and Luke, led by the Spirit of God, wrote their Gospels and added other materials.

The book of Matthew was written to Jews, by a Jew, to instruct Gentile converts. If you look in the last chapter, Matthew 28:19,20, you get a clue that Matthew became the instructor, and that Jesus' Great Commission was that the church of Jesus Christ go out and win and disciple and teach all the things that had been entrusted to Matthew. So the book of Matthew is both a Gospel and a teaching book; Gospel in the sense that it records a history of the people of God, but primarily the ministry of Jesus Christ.

Some commentaries on Matthew call the Gospel of Matthew the New Testament Pentateuch. The Pentateuch of the Old Testament refers to the five books of Moses—Genesis, Exodus, Leviticus, Numbers and Deuteronomy, and since Matthew's Gospel is divided into five sections, each one ending with the phrase, "When Jesus had ended these sayings," some see a parallel. I don't entirely buy that opinion.

The commentaries also say that the 12 apostles are patterned after the 12 tribes, to again maintain a parallel. I think that is true.

But they also say that the Sermon on the Mount began when Jesus "saw the multitudes," and "went up on the mountains" and there He gave a new law, just as Moses went up on Mount Sinai to get the original law. Well, that's interesting, but I don't think it is right. The Sermon on the Mount is not the new law. It is a new life, a completely different way of looking at things.

The Sermon on the Mount

Was the information which Matthew recorded in chapters 5, 6 and 7 all contained in one sermon preached at one time? Or did Matthew bring together all of Jesus' teachings and lump them into one thing he calls a sermon?

I believe it was a sermon, all preached on that mountain in Galilee on that particular occasion. I believe it, because of what Matthew records before and after the sermon. In chapter 5:1 we read, "And when He saw the multitudes, He went up on the mountain; and after He sat down, His disciples came to Him." Chapter 7:28,29 concludes: "The result was that when Jesus had finished these words, the multitudes were amazed at His teaching; for He was teaching them as one having authority, and not as their scribes." It seems that what Matthew is saying is that the discourse had a beginning and it had a conclusion; it was an entire sermon.

Then why does Luke record the same information in 10 different sections of his Gospel? In my opinion, Luke records these teachings as Jesus continued to teach them on different occasions. But on this one occasion, Jesus took His disciples aside. The multitudes gathered around Him and His disciples and Jesus taught all of these things, bringing them together in one magnificent sermon, the Sermon on the Mount.

Now some have said it isn't really a sermon because

it only takes 10 minutes to preach it. I tried it, and even if I move rather slowly, getting kind of excited at certain points, it only takes about 12 minutes. Dr. Robert G. Lee used to say, "Sermonettes are preached by preacherettes and they produce Christianettes." So, he contended, the longer the sermon, the more godly the people.

I believe the Sermon on the Mount is a summary of what Jesus taught on that mountain. When He went through the Beatitudes, it is very possible that Jesus said, "Blessed are . . ." and then went on to interpret each one in great detail. However, we have in these three chapters what the Spirit of God wanted all of us to have, complete, the major thrusts of the sermon. It may originally have taken Jesus more than an hour to preach it in its entirety.

The Sermon on the Mount is not an "interim ethic." Albert Schweitzer was a great musician, a gifted doctor and a frequently deficient theologian. Schweitzer said that Jesus thought the end of the age was to come very, very quickly. Therefore, He gave the Sermon on the Mount as an interim ethic. In essence he said, "We just have a little while left and so it's going to take some radical living. During this radical period here is what you are going to do . . ." Schweitzer was wrong. There is no intimation that Jesus thought the end of the age was so imminent. Nor is there any suggestion that His sermon was intended for just a short period during a crisis.

The Sermon on the Mount is not a banner for the "social gospel." At the turn of the century and early in the twentieth century certain clergymen introduced us to the social gospel. It was a great movement in the sense that it was widespread, not in the sense that it was correct. The social gospel movement was challenged by fundamentalists in the early twentieth century, provoking some great controversies. The philosophy of the proponents of the social gospel—men like Walter Rauschenbusch (*Theology of the Social Gospel*), Washington Gladden, Harry Emerson Fosdick and others—was that if you take the Sermon on the Mount, seriously believe it and practice it, you will bring the Kingdom of God into our world and there will be no more wars, strife, conflicts, poverty, and so on. That sounded good, but they were wrong. There is no way people can live a Christian life without being converted.

The advent of World War I shot holes all through the social gospel theology. Along came Karl Barth and his brand of neo-orthodoxy shot some more holes in it. Today the social gospel movement is dead as it can be. Obviously, as long as there are sinners, a social gospel will not work.

The Sermon on the Mount is not "legalism." Again we have the idea that Jesus gave us a "new law" on the mount to replace the "old law" of Moses. The Sermon on the Mount is not a new law—it is a new life. Jesus often said things like, "You have heard that it was said," then followed up with, "but, I say to you." Or "It was said," then, "but I say to you." Or "You have heard, but I say." With these statements Jesus is saying, "What you have believed is the law; what I am giving you is a new life." The old law was "legalism," but Jesus said, "I bring you a new life." This new life can only be introduced by a new birth; a new law can never do what God can do through a new birth.

The Sermon on the Mount is not "impractical idealism." Those who contend that the Sermon on the Mount is impractical reason that to let someone slap you across the face and then turn the other cheek so he can slap you again is unreasonable. We don't live this way, they say. We can't live this way. We can't be people who live without anxieties—it's part of modern-day life to be anxious. It's impractical to try not to be anxious. Everybody is supposed to have anxieties. What do you mean, love your enemies? What kind of national defense program is that? The people who cannot accept the Sermon on the Mount on the grounds that its impractical idealism say that it may be practical for some but certainly not for normal people.

God would not give us something that couldn't work. If He calls us to do it, He'll provide the grace and Spirit to allow us to do it. I say it's illegitimate for people to lop off any Scriptures they cannot accept. Second Timothy 3:16 says that "*all* Scripture is given by God and inspired by God and is profitable for doctrine, reproof, for correction and instruction." Again, in Matthew 28:20, in *Phillips* version, when Jesus commissioned us to teach "them to observe *all* that I commanded you," He didn't intend for anyone to cut out three chapters of Matthew, the Sermon on the Mount, and call them "impractical."

The Sermon on the Mount is not "reserved for the future age." The original Scofield Bible notes said that Jesus did not intend this sermon to be for the church, nor is it to be lived out by the church; rather it is for the kingdom age—the future age. The notes for the new Scofield Bible have been revised and now say that the Sermon on the Mount is for our age.

There are two major reasons why we know that Jesus intended this sermon for us. First, there is no place in the text where it says that Jesus' words are to be put in a holding pattern. The Bible doesn't say that *someday* you are going to do this, but always gives the impression you are to do it *now:* Today you are the "salt of the earth"; today you are the "light of the world"; today you walk a "narrow path"; today you "build your house upon the rock"; today "blessed are the poor in spirit." That's today. No intimation of their being for some future day. In fact, the Sermon gives all kinds of what we call present-tense imperatives: do it now, do it now—rejoice today; swear not now; go now; give now; give heed now. All those are for now—right now, not for some future kingdom age.

The second reason we know the Sermon is for today

is that these chapters don't sound like the millennium age. Can you imagine a millennium that has the problem described in Matthew 5:11, "Blessed are you when men revile you, and persecute you, and say all kinds of evil against you falsely, on account of Me"? In the kingdom age there's not going to be that problem. Also in chapter 5, verses 38 and 39 it says, "You have heard that it was said, 'An eye for an eye, and a tooth for a tooth.' But I say to you, do not resist him who is evil; but whoever slaps you on your right cheek, turn to him the other also." There's no slapping of cheeks in the millennium. You won't have to go around turning the other cheek. The millennium will be a kingdom of righteousness when it comes. Chapter 6, verse 19: "Do not lay up for yourselves treasures upon earth, where moth and rust destroy, and where thieves break in and steal." You won't need an alarm system during the millennium to keep out the thieves.

Do you know what these three chapters of the Sermon remind us of? Today's *Los Angeles Times*. We are in a world full of bad tax collectors, unjust officials, hypocrites, thieves, false prophets, people going around slapping you on the face. That's the front page of today's newspaper, not the millennium. The Sermon on the Mount addresses people who live in our kind of world.

The Sermon on the Mount is a call for new birth. You may read it and say, "Hey, I'd like to live that way," and you go out and try to live that way, and it just doesn't work. So you get frustrated and you say, "Baumann's laid another bomb on us. It's wrong. It's good to study but it just doesn't work out in the marketplace. There is no way I can be all this on the Santa Ana Freeway." Well, if you can't live the new life of the Sermon on the Mount, then let's work at it.

This text drives us to the cross. It makes us realize how unjust, how selfish, how carnal, how needy we really are, and it drives us in desperation to the foot of the cross, recognizing that everything in the Sermon is impossible without a new birth and the power of the Spirit of God. We don't go around passing this sermon out to unbelievers. It is not something unbelievers can practice. Living the Sermon on the Mount begins when you bow in penitence and faith and receive Jesus Christ as Saviour and Lord. It will never work outside of the new birth. It reminds us that we have to start at the cross.

The Sermon on the Mount is a call to new life. It shows the conflict between the church and the carnal, secular world. When you start to live the way the Sermon tells you, all of a sudden you're unique. One person has suggested that the key verse of the whole sermon is, "Therefore, do not be like them" (Matt. 6:8). He's right.

To many observers the most obvious feature of today's church is its superficiality. We are so much like the world that we have become absorbed by it. The world has come into the church and the church has become worldly, so that it no longer has a cutting edge, no longer has a strong, vibrant, clear-cut testimony. We've just kind of got caught up with it, and we move along with the stream. Romans 12:2 talks about us: "Do not be conformed to this world, but be transformed." As *Phillips* said it, "Do not let the world squeeze you into its mold."

What we need to do is move through the Sermon, pop out of the mold and say, "Hey, here is a new life, here is a distinctive life, here is a life that is a contrast."

The great word of the Sermon on the Mount is simply this—we are to be different! Not peculiar, not strange, but unique. Qualitatively distinctive. "Therefore, do not be like them."

The contrast all through this sermon is: Here are "them," here are we; here are they, here are we; here are those who don't know our Lord, here are those who do; here are those who are carnal, here are those who take it seriously.

The Sermon on the Mount is a call to a *blessed*, distinctive, qualitatively better life. All the way through it says, "Blessed are . . . Blessed are . . . Blessed are . . . ," which means *happy are* . . . The happiest people in the world ought to be Christians. Blessed—happy—are those who know our Lord; serene, confident, content, peaceful, joyful, soul-satisfied—that deep sense of soul confidence. We rest in our Lord and we're a people who experience contentment. If you want to get blessed, this is the place to get it.

The Sermon on the Mount describes a life fit for a king. One day Solomon was sitting in the palace and he looked out the window and said, "I have seen slaves riding on horses and princes walking like slaves on the land" (Eccles. 10:7). He said, "Look, there are the princes—they're playing servants, and the servants are playing prince. The whole world has gone topsy turvy." And Solomon said, "What in the world is going on in my world."

There are two marching orders given to the church. In Genesis it says, "You are to *go* into the world and *have dominion*" (see 1:28). Do you know what dominion is? You are to reign. The people of God are to take over as kings. And then Paul says, "Reign in life through the One, Jesus Christ" (Rom. 5:17). You were called to reign, you were called to kingliness—as the people of the Kingdom. Are you marching along playing servant or are you riding along in the regal life as one who has the distinctive experience of living in the Sermon on the Mount? Are you walking or are you riding? You ought to be riding as one who is fit for the king, as one who is experiencing dominion and reigning through Jesus Christ.

The Challenge to Your Life

Each chapter will conclude with a section entitled, "The Challenge to Your Life." It is possible that your challenge for this chapter is to say, "I finally need to make my peace with God. The life described in the

Sermon on the Mount is impossible because I've never even trusted Christ as my Saviour. Today I am going to receive Christ as my Saviour." You can do that right now and begin to experience this new life described in the Sermon on the Mount. Will you trust Him?

If you are a Christian, here is your chance to get up and begin to ride like a king, to experience a counterculture that is a life of blessedness and great joy. The Sermon on the Mount was not given to us simply to edify us or to satisfy our intellectual curiosity; it was given to us to be obeyed.

The instructor in the traffic school I told you about at the beginning of this chapter said something else that made a lasting impression on me. He said, "Eighty percent of you will never be the same after taking this class. You will probably always buckle your seat belt and be a better driver. But 20 percent of you will remain unchanged." That's the way it is in life. Some people will hear the truth and remain unchanged. The Beatitudes were given by Jesus so that our lives would be challenged and we would change.

I challenge you to not only hear the Word and reflect upon it, but to allow the Holy Spirit to "flesh it out" in your experience. As my old professor of Christian education used to say, "The best binding for a Bible is not Morocco, but human flesh."

For Further Study

1. The title of this chapter is "Christian Counter-

Culture." How does this message of the Beatitudes relate to this title? What is the Christian counterculture?

2. Recall Dr. Boice's comment that no one can realistically live up to the standards set by Christ in the Beatitudes. If the principles laid forth in the Beatitudes are so impossible to follow, why should we even try?

3. What challenge to life do the Beatitudes pose for you?

CHAPTER TWO

Meant for Sinners

Matthew 5:3

Only sinners are allowed to read this chapter. If you qualify, you're welcome to continue. Paul said to Timothy, "It is a trustworthy statement, deserving full acceptance, that Christ Jesus came into the world to save sinners, among whom I am foremost of all. And yet for this reason I found mercy, in order that in me as the foremost, Jesus Christ might demonstrate His perfect patience, as an example for those who would believe in Him for eternal life" (1 Tim. 1:15,16).

Jesus has climbed the mount. He's sitting on a large red rock and the wind is cleaning the air on the top of the mountain as He begins to teach. His first word is, "Blessed." All of a sudden the multitude pays attention. The listeners kind of rise up—there's good news ahead. And indeed there was.

Each of the Beatitudes, and there are eight of them, follows the same formula: (1) There is always a condition, and it's what Jesus calls a blessing—blessed is the one who . . . We are blessed if we accept whatever responsibility follows. (2) With each responsibility comes a privilege. In the Beatitude we are studying in this chapter (Matt. 5:3) the condition is "Blessed are the poor in spirit." The privilege is "for theirs is the kingdom of heaven." Thirteen words; 12 in the original Greek.

Blessedness, a Coveted Possession

There is a frantic thirst for blessing, for happiness in our modern world. I see people scurrying through life in a mad, mad quest for happiness. They look in all kinds of places—on the beaches, in places of entertainment, in power, authority, fame, money—whatever. There is a mad desire to be happy.

Billy Graham's book, *Secret of Happiness* is, at the time I am writing this, in its fourteenth printing—most books never make it past the first. This fact indicates the hunger people have for happiness. In his book he talks about a famous film actress, whom he chooses not to identify, who said: "I have money, beauty, glamour, popularity—I should be the happiest woman in the world and I'm miserable." People all over the world are scurrying after what she has, hanging on with breaking fingernails, wanting somehow to experience her kind of "happiness." Those who obtain this position are kind of a unique people; they are in a coveted position; they have something most of us don't have.

But the kind of happiness—or blessedness—of which Jesus is speaking is not *what we experience* as much as *who we are*. It's not primarily what happens to us that matters; it's the fact that God is saying we are highly favored. The word *blessed* means "highly favored, set aside, distinguished for favor, honored." We are a people who have been blessed by God.

One book says that the Beatitudes are Jesus' view of emotional health; they are a formula for mental health, and He presents eight characteristics of happy, well-adjusted people. Well, that kind of misses what the text is really all about. What the text says is that these people are favored folks whom God has blessed, has honored, has distinguished with blessing. To be sure there is a personal experience of happiness. When you are favored by God and respond to Him you do have a happiness within you. But this might be a superficial happiness, very temporary. The "blessed" of the Beatitudes is a deep, soul contentment. It is something that is resident within, deeply spiritual, not right at the surface of our experience. It does not come and go very quickly. It is the kind of thing that buoys us up at the heart of our being. It is a deep spiritual contentment.

Now to be sure, there are those very happy moments all of us experience that aren't necessarily spiritual, and don't be afraid of those moments. One night my son Steve and I were watching something on television. It was a singing dog contest. I laughed so hard I cried. We woke up my wife Nancy with our laughter and she came out to see what was going on in her home. Now that's kind of superficial, but we shouldn't be afraid of this kind of happiness; we need to laugh. But this is not the "happiness" Jesus is speaking of. When He says "Blessed are," He's talking about something that is a gift of the Holy Spirit.

Jesus, of course, had this gift. He was a man of sorrows and He was blessed. God had favored Him objectively and subjectively; He was a man who was at peace, who had deep, deep contentment. When you experience what the Beatitudes are all about you will know that God also has honored you. You will know the joy of God's favor. You will know what it is to be happy—to have godly contentment.

One day I was standing in line at one of those fast-food chicken places. Right behind me stood a lady—I don't think she was five feet tall. She was well along in years and dressed in the dowdiest clothes I have ever seen. Her dress looked as if it had come out of an antique shop. It had a lot of strange colors in it and just kind of hung on her. She had on a wig and on top of that a big floppy hat. On her feet were two woolen socks—one blue and one gray, and a pair of men's shoes at least four sizes too large for her. She turned around and they didn't even move. She kind of sloshed along in her shoes. But she was the happiest person I've seen in a long time. She was having a great time. She kidded me about my order, which wasn't really that funny, and she kidded the folks behind her. She was so happy and joyful. I gave my order and stepped aside as she joked with the man when she gave her order. She didn't order much—she obviously didn't have much money.

Also in line were a couple, husband and wife, and their child—well dressed. They were really "with-it" people. They just kind of looked over at her, and all of us said to ourselves, in chorus, "That's kind of pathetic, isn't it?" And then almost immediately I thought, "But you know there are a lot of 'with-it' people who are very unhappy."

Happiness is not ever related to the clothes you wear, the cash in your pocket, the house you enjoy making payments on monthly—none of those things. Ultimately, all this is really quite superficial, and truly happy people may have very minimal means or very significant means. But the blessing which God favors us with is something we experience secondarily—a deep spiritual contentment.

And who is it for? For those who are "poor in spirit."

Poverty, a Commendable Position

"Are you kidding? What's so good about being poor?"

The word that is translated "poor" appears about 34 times in the New Testament, and every time it appears it's contrasted to wealth. The rich, young ruler is told to go out and sell what he has and give to the "poor" and you get the picture that *poor* means "one who is with-

out." Yet this text in Matthew 5:3 has the audacity to
say, "Blessed are the poor in spirit." And if that misses
you, look over in Luke where it's translated, "Blessed
are you who are poor" (Luke 6:20). What's so good
about being poor?

Now I'm not a great Sophie Tucker fan. In fact, I
know very little about Sophie Tucker. But in an interview she once disclosed that she had had a very poor
childhood; of course she became very prosperous as an
actress. In the interview they asked, "As you look back
on it, weren't those good days when you didn't have
much?" She replied, "Listen, I've been rich and I've
been poor and believe me rich is better."

When Jesus said, "Blessed are the poor," He was
not talking about material poverty. If He had been, how
would we respond to all of those passages that talk about
giving to those who are needy, those who have not? If
Jesus had been talking about material poverty, that there
is blessing in being poor, our response should be to keep
them in a position where they can receive such a blessing. Don't push those poor people out of the path of
God's favor by giving to them, for to be rich is to be
deprived of joy and deep contentment. So, let's keep
them in a position where they have not; therefore, they
will receive joy. "It would undercut the whole process of
ministry to the needy which God has called us to if we
interpreted "poor" to mean material poverty. We'd be
foolish to support the "boat people." We'd be out of the
will of God to give to any kind of ministry that lifts people

who are hurting financially and materially, because blessed are the materially poor.

What does the Old Testament teach about this kind of poor? Look in Zephaniah 3:12: "But I will leave among you a humble and lowly [poor] people, and they will take refuge in the name of the Lord." The words for "poor" in the Hebrew gradually underwent a change of meaning. They began by meaning just "poor," but gradually progressed until the Hebrew words meant "so poor" that the poor had no other alternative but to put his whole trust in God. The words took on spiritual overtones. This passage in Zephaniah uses "poor" (or "lowly" in *NASB*) to mean one who is so humble and poor that he has no other recourse except to completely depend on God. It is this person who finds that he really does not have any resources and must throw himself completely upon God; he is inadequate within himself; therefore, he turns to God.

In Psalm 34:6, "This poor man cried and the Lord heard him; and saved him out of all his troubles." The *New American Standard Bible* has a margin note indicating that the word "poor" can also be translated "afflicted." Here is a man who is afflicted and unable to save himself, and he looks outside of himself to God for salvation and to meet his needs. A "poor" man then is one who, when he looks inside, finds need. So he looks to God and finds his need met. Afflicted, unable to save himself, he looks to God.

Isaiah 41:17 says that "the afflicted and needy are

seeking water." "Afflicted" in the *New American Standard Bible* has a margin note that says "afflicted" also means "poor." "The *poor* and needy are seeking water, but there is none, and their tongue is parched with thirst; I the Lord will answer them Myself, as the God of Israel I will not forsake them. I will open rivers on the bare heights, and springs in the midst of the valleys; I will make the wilderness a pool of water, and the dry land fountains of water" (vv. 17, 18). This speaks of a spiritual poverty here, and it's almost commended. On the other side is the reality that this spiritual poverty is matched with the riches and provision of God. Poor is spiritual need, and the riches that God provides are spiritual.

What does God require for us to receive spiritual riches? Look in Isaiah 57. The riches of God are given to those who are poor. Who are the poor? "For thus says the high and exalted One who lives forever, whose name is Holy, I dwell on a high and holy place, and also with the contrite and lowly of spirit in order to revive the spirit of the lowly and to revive the heart of the contrite" (v. 15). Who are the folks that God favors? The lowly and contrite who recognize their own spiritual need.

This is affirmed further in Isaiah 66:1, 2: "Thus says the Lord, 'Heaven is My throne, and the earth is My footstool. Where then is a house you could build for Me? And where is a place that I may rest? For My hand made all these things, thus all these things came into being,' declares the Lord. 'But to this one I will look, to him who is humble and contrite of spirit, and who trembles at My word.' " What is our conclusion? Simply this, that although "poor" in the Old Testament may have started out as a description of a person's situation, it developed into a description of the poverty of our spiritual lives. When we are humble and contrite and recognize our condition, then God will favor us and meet our need. So the principle is simply this: To be poor in spirit is to acknowledge our spiritual poverty, our spiritual bankruptcy before God. That's it. Even if we believe we are strong and secure before God, outside of His grace we are bankrupt. That's what it means to be poor in spirit.

Poverty in the New Testament

The New Testament discusses not only some of the possibilities of living this kind of life, it also tells of some dangers.

First, it is easy to become self-deceived about our poverty of spirit, about spiritual bankruptcy. We can somehow forget who we really are. In Revelation 3:17, the angel is talking to the church at Laodicea: "Because you say, 'I am rich, and have become wealthy, and have need of nothing,' and you do not know that you are wretched and miserable and poor and blind and naked." Just about the time I am feeling good and I'm telling the Lord how well-to-do I am, that I'm spiritually well off, the Lord comes along and says, "You are wicked and you're wretched and you're naked." All of a sudden! How did I ever get deceived?

One reason we get deceived is that we tend to find our standards and our norms by looking at other people. When we do that, we look pretty good. If you compare yourself to the man who has no faith in God, who hasn't any moral scruples, who just kind of wings it through life, you may say, "Hey, I'm doing all right. I'm pretty well, spiritually, and I am in good shape." Then the Lord comes along and says you are naked and miserable, you're wretched and you've been deceived.

One of the saddest stories in the Bible is the story of Samson and Delilah. Remember the story? Samson was the "incredible hulk" of the Old Testament, a man who had all kinds of strength. But, he also had Delilah, who was a deceitful woman. Delilah tried to discover the secret of Samson's strength. If she could just find the secret of his strength, the Philistines could move in and take over for Samson was the oppressor of the Philistines. She asked him his secret. And for a while he played games with her. But one day, in a moment of weakness, this big hunk of a man said, "It's my hair. If you cut my hair I'll become soft as a grape." Modern translation—not very strong. He went to sleep on her lap—I can just see him purring away as Delilah strokes his lovely locks. As soon as he's asleep, she calls in someone who clips off his hair. Then Delilah says, "Samson, the Philistines have come." And he wakes up, "I'll get them." "But he did not know that the Lord had departed from him" (Judg. 16:20). He was weak, miserable and spiritually naked.

We play those Samson games. Then a problem comes along and we move right on in and suddenly discover that the Lord has departed from us. We thought we were rich, but really we were poor. And we are no longer in a position to go forth in battle, in conquest, in victory, because we have been deceived. And we thought we were doing so well; we were so strong. But God's grace and His blessing are to those who say, "I am poor and bankrupt." They are the ones who are paradoxically rich. But, self-deception is very easy.

Not only can we become self-deceived about our spiritual poverty, *we can also become self-righteous.*

Romans 3:10 says, "There is none righteous"; verse 20 of the same chapter says, "By the works of the Law no flesh will be justified." Verse 23 says, "All have sinned and fall short of the glory of God." That's us. *All.* I started this chapter by saying, "Only sinners are allowed to read this chapter." Well, I guess you're still with me, because you know we all qualify. No question about it, all we can propose before God; every way we can commend ourselves to God; all those little recitals of our virtue are all unacceptable.

Remember the story of the two men who went to the Temple to pray? One was a Pharisee. He said "to himself, 'God, I thank Thee that I am not like other people.' " He kind of looks around and there's this fellow over in the corner beating his chest, and saying, "God, be merciful to me, the sinner!" Then the Pharisee says, "I thank you that I am not like this tax-gatherer" (see Luke 18:10-14). Spiritual pride is contrary to the standards of God. We may not be as blatant about our spirituality as the Pharisee was; but we may tend, very quietly within our beings, to kind of puff up our chests and say, "We're doing all right. When I look at others around me; when I look at my neighbors; when I look at the people I work with, God's really got something special in me."

Self-righteousness is unacceptable.

The greatest possibility in this business of living with spiritual bankruptcy is that *self-emptying is redemptive.* When you empty yourself and throw yourself open to God, then you realize that you are a candidate for His grace. Luke 18:14 says, "Every one who exalts himself shall be humbled, but he who humbles himself shall be exalted." The very minute we go down God says, "Now I can use you." When you say, "I am weak and I am poor and I am wretched and I am bankrupt," God will step in. Jesus had nothing to do with the self-righteous of His day who professed to be righteous.

The way to redemption is to recognize that when you are spiritually bankrupt, yours is the kingdom of heaven.

The Kingdom of Heaven

"Blessed are the poor in spirit, for theirs is the kingdom of heaven." God takes up His reign in those who acknowledge their poverty. And our citizenship is a Christian privilege. "The kingdom" is a reference to the reign of God in your heart. The moment you humble yourself and pour out your heart to God and recognize that you are spiritually bankrupt and receive Him into your life, then the King of kings comes and sets up His throne in your heart. Now to be sure, there is a day coming when God will set up His earthly kingdom. But right now, in the heart of every single believer is a throne upon which the King of kings reigns.

The first step for receiving the kingdom of heaven is to acknowledge your poverty; to say there is no way you are going to satisfy God's standards. To compare your life with others and to reason that you are doing "all right" is not enough. You have to do as Isaiah did when in the presence of Holy God he said, "Holy, Holy, Holy, is the Lord of hosts, the whole earth is full of His glory" (Isa. 6:3). When he went away he was saying, "Woe is me, for I am ruined! Because I am a man of unclean lips" (v. 5). Many of us tend to say "Yeah is me" when we compare ourselves with others. When we can say "Woe is me," then His favor and His kingdom take place. God comes in to reign in the life of the one who says, "I'm bankrupt. I look in my spiritual checkbook and my account's closed. I've nothing."

The next step is to accept His riches, as if we were

beggars coming to a Holy God. Then He receives us and offers us all the riches of Himself. The songwriter put it so beautifully: "Nothing in my hand I bring, simply to Thy cross I cling."[1]

The Challenge to Your Life

One of my favorite writers is John Powell, a Jesuit priest and professor of psychology at Loyola University in Chicago. He is the author of numerous books including one entitled *Unconditional Love*. Many years ago Powell was in Germany studying the German language. While he was there he was called to be the chaplain of a little Bavarian convent. He says that he was given a sister who would come and clean and maintain his room—84 years old. The minute he would step out of his room she came in, dusted everything, waxed the floor, polished the furniture, straightened out every wrinkle. Polish, shine, buff, take out wrinkles—she was compulsive.

He says that one day he just stepped out of the room to take a little walk and when he came back, there was *schwester*, "sister." She was on her knees putting a little more shine on another coat of wax. He said, "Sister, you work too much." Sister stood up, looked at him with a sincerity that bordered on severity and said simply, "Listen, heaven isn't cheap, you know." As Powell says, she was a dear lady but she had missed it. He adds, "God is not a Shylock demanding his pound of flesh for eternal life."

Salvation is given to those who are spiritually bankrupt and who pray, "There's nothing I can do to satisfy you; but you've done it through Jesus Christ. I accept it all."

Have you acknowledged your spiritual bankruptcy? Have you accepted God's riches in personal salvation? You can do that right now!

"Blessed are the poor in spirit."

For Further Study

1. Who are the "poor" Christ speaks of in the first Beatitude? What does God require for us to receive spiritual riches?

2. It is easy to become self-deceived about our poverty of spirit. How is it that we can become deceived?

3. As Christians we can also become self-righteous. How does the believer correct this attitude? What are some ways of preventing the attitude of self-righteousness?

Notes
1. Augustus M. Toplady, "Rock of Ages, Cleft for Me," verse 3.
2. John Powell, *Unconditional Love* (Niles, IL: Argus Communication, 1978), p. 10.

CHAPTER THREE

A Time to Mourn

Matthew 5:4

In one of the great psalms of David, after he has just rehearsed his disappointments, his discouragement, his crises, virtually the whole bottoming out of his life, he utters the following words: "O that I had wings like a dove! I would fly away and be at rest" (Ps. 55:6). Ever feel that way? Ever feel that the pressure has reached the maximum in your own pressure cooker and you're about ready to whistle? That you can't take any more, and you'd like to fly away and be at rest, away from it all? It seems many of us live that kind of life and have the kind of pressures where we are anxious, when we encounter crises and discouragement and disappointment.

It is in this context that Jesus addresses the Beatitude, "Blessed are those who mourn, for they shall be comforted" (Matt. 5:4). Solomon in Ecclesiastes 3:1, 4, said, "There is an appointed time for everything. . . . A time to weep, and a time to laugh; a time to mourn, and a time to dance." Strangely, the Bible portrays the "time to mourn" as paradoxically a happy time.

Paradox of Christian Experience

"Blessed are those who mourn?" we say. "Oh, no. No way—nonsense. What kind of an upside-down world is that?" One man translated this text, "Happy are the unhappy." How in the world are you happy when you're unhappy? Yet Jesus has the audacity to suggest a paradox, because usually when we are happy things are really upside down rather than downside up. We're happy when things are positive and encouraging. By nature, just naturally, we are happy when we receive recognition, when we're recognized and when something is done to acknowledge who we are. When we get an award, a trophy, some praise—all of a sudden we feel happy, we feel good about ourselves. But when we're forgotten, when we feel alone and shut out from everybody, that's miserable.

We're also happy when we win a battle, whether it's playing tennis or selling a car or making a good grade at school—that's winning the battle. We like that. We like to come out on top, victorious. Show me a good loser and I'll show you a loser. Nothing very happy about that. We want to win. It's the Little League syndrome: "Let's win!" It carries over into all of life. "Let's win!" And when we lose, we're miserable. One pastor said in his sermon, "You may beat me at Ping-Pong and I may smile on the outside, but I'll never forget it." He talked about a staff member who played him in Ping-Pong, and the pastor beat the other fellow by one point. He said, "That's the closest he ever came to getting fired!" Win! Sure, we're happy when we win, and miserable when we lose.

We're also happy when we're in control of things; when everything is kind of domesticated, this is in place and that is in place. But when everything that matters is blowing in the wind and the only things we have under control are things that aren't important, then we're miserable.

We're also happy when somehow we can deny a certain reality, when we can camouflage all the difficulties around us; gloss them over, put a frosting over them, deny the pressures and problems and live without acknowledging them. It's that "eat, drink and be merry" spirit. You remember the little song that says: "What's the use of worrying, it never was worthwhile; so pack up your troubles in your old kit bag and smile, smile, smile"? What that is saying is, "I'm going to hide all the unpleasant things and go around looking like a Cheshire cat and smile, moving through life as if they don't exist. Pack it all up in the old kit bag and smile, smile, smile. That's kind of a denial of reality, to camouflage what is really hurting us, as if life only has a time to laugh, only a time to dance. But the text says that there's also a time to cry and a time to mourn, and the Bible has the audacity to say, in the words of Jesus, that you can be happy even then. You can be blessed. There's the paradox of the text, that at the very time when we should not be, by the grace of God we can be.

What does it mean to mourn? The word *mourn* is a strong word. It means "intense sorrow." It is a kind of emotion that is often expressed externally, when you weep and lament, and you're shaken by something. It's not the kind of a wave that goes over you that says things aren't going well. When you mourn, your whole body gets involved in it. Your body may shake, you may cry, your whole insides begin to turn, and you're deeply caught up in the emotion. It's the strongest word the Greeks had to describe sorrow. It was the word they used to describe what people went through when they lost their closest loved ones. You bottom out, you're torn, and you weep, and you lament. You've gone through it. Jesus says you can be happy when you mourn. How do you handle that? How do you put that all together?

Problems of the Human Experience

I'm going to suggest two problems about which we mourn: (1) personal loss, and (2) personal sin.

Personal loss is when someone who has shared your life is simply wrenched out of your clutches and you are left to stand alone. A parent, a mate, a child, one who has walked with you is now gone, and you walk alone. You have a deep sense of personal loss. That's a time to mourn.

When Abraham lost his dear wife, he wept bitterly. When David lost his beloved son Absalom, even though his son had turned on him, he wept bitterly. When Jeremiah looked out over that great city and saw the people going into exile, he wept bitterly. He was losing something very dear to him. Tears, lamenting and mourning are necessary and natural. There's nothing unnatural about tears.

I think it's tragic that we train boys not to cry. We feel somehow that tears are reserved for only half of society—they're for ladies. When a little boy cries we say, "Be a man. Men don't cry." The little kid is hurting but on the outside he begins to play this role he's got to play the rest of his life. He gets tough. Tears on the inside, but he plays tough on the outside. That's tragic! Now I'm not sure all of you ladies are prepared to handle a bunch of men who weep, but it would be better for us if we learned a little bit more about doing it. It's a natural expression that God has given us. Tears are a gift of God to purge us, to cleanse us, to let that deep, intense emotion come out and begin the process of healing.

There's no weakness in tears. Jesus cried—the strongest of men who ever walked down the dusty roads of Palestine or any other place on earth, who was a man among men—Jesus wept openly and deeply when He looked over Jerusalem, a city that broke His heart because they were in unbelief. He wept at the tomb of

Lazarus, not because He thought Lazarus would not come alive, but because of the sin that brought death to the whole world. Jesus was not afraid of tears.

Tears are part of that whole healing process which enables us to accept the loss of somebody, to accept life when a loved one is gone. Tears help us work our way back. They help us go through that grieving period; they're a very natural, healing part of grief. If grief is not expressed, if it isn't ventilated, if it isn't lanced, it eats away on the inside of us and builds up to a boil, emotionally and spiritually. We must allow grief to be released. I've seen people who refused to accept that they could cry and still be a man or a woman. Somehow they thought that death of a loved one was a time for heroics. This is a time when they could show strength and come on like champions!

I've also heard people say to a mourner, "You know he's better off now that he's with the Lord. Stop crying." Don't deny tears. Death is like an amputation. Something very special is gone all of a sudden and the bereaved is going to limp. He or she needs the catharsis, the healing of letting it out. Encourage those around you who are in grief to go all the way through it. Don't short-circuit it.

Don't be afraid to go through a mourning period. Don't be afraid to weep. Don't be afraid to let God cleanse your inward being through mourning and grieving and tears. It's all part of the process of restoration to life anew.

Personal loss, however, is the secondary meaning of the text, "Blessed are those who mourn." Almost in concert, all biblical scholars say that this verse does not refer primarily to mourning over personal loss; *rather it refers to mourning over personal sin,* the kind of deep grieving I do over sin in my life. Remember verse 3, "Blessed are the poor in spirit"? We discovered that one who is poor in spirit is one who looks into his life and says, "I am bankrupt spiritually. I have nothing in my account. I am thrust upon the grace of God. I need God." To be poor in spirit is to acknowledge your spiritual bankruptcy. Then you become a candidate for His riches and His grace.

Quite naturally, then, when you accept your bankruptcy you move to do something about it; you mourn because of that condition. You mourn over the sin in your life. You mourn over your failure to have righteousness and holiness and purity in your life. From the time when you accept your spiritual poverty until you mourn over it is the process of confession and contrition which leads to salvation, healing and restoration.

There has only been one baby born on earth who was not a sinner at birth—the Lord Jesus Christ. I never found it necessary to go to the hospital baby ward and say, "Now kids, here is how you can act like your parents. Here is how you can be sinful, selfish, and prideful. We're going to give you a short course in it because the rest of us have already mastered it." A newborn baby hits the earth as a sinner. By nature we are that way. David said, "In sin did my mother conceive me" (Ps. 51:5, *KJV*). He didn't mean it was an illicit relationship, of course. He meant that he came into the world with a bent in that direction. Adam and Eve distorted the whole thing right at the roots.

You may say, "Well, if I had had a chance, I would have done differently."

No, you wouldn't. You'd have done the same thing Adam and Eve did. Even if you had not been born a sinner, you would end up one; we all practice being sinners—by choice, not only by birth. Even if you deny the doctrine of original sin, you still end up doing that which is sinful. The Word of God tells us that this life-style we have adopted calls for penitence and mourning and grieving over what we are doing. When we can mourn over our sins we begin the process of turning. Now, it's hard to admit that we are sinners. We've tried to train each other not to admit our weakness, our failure, our sin; but admission and repentance are the way to happiness, the way to healing, the way to restoration. The way to joy in the Christian life is through the process of genuine sorrow for sin.

Now, once you recognize that you are a sinner there are all kinds of ways to handle it:

1. You can admit it and try to do better on your own. Have you ever tried that? Isn't it a bummer? It doesn't work.

2. You can try to deny it. The Pharisees did that. They lived a masquerade, denying that they were sin-

ners underneath. God looked at them as whited sepulchers (see Matt. 23:27).

3. You can do as some have done—despair over it. Say, "What's the use?" Or

4. You can do what the text suggests, and that is turn to God, which is repentance. The word *repent* in Greek means "to turn." When you come to an understanding of who you are and you genuinely accept your spiritual bankruptcy—which is to be poor in spirit—and then you mourn—which is contrition and a genuine sorrow for your sin—then you're ready to receive the healing and the cleansing and to be made whole. That's when the happiness comes.

When was the last time you cried over personal sin? When was the last time you were deeply moved over the sin in your life? Have you thought it easier to cry when you watch "Love Boat"? Or the soap operas in the afternoon? Or dramatic films? Or do you allow the Spirit of God to reveal yourself as you really are and drive you to grieving over your personal sin? That's the way to healing. That's the way to vitality. That's the way to spirituality. That's the initial way to salvation.

Peace of the Believer's Experience

The last part of Matthew 5:4 says, "They shall be comforted." That's the promise. "Blessed [happy] are those who mourn, for they shall be comforted." Now here is where it becomes gospel and positive. What does it mean to be comforted? *Comfort* comes from two Latin words which mean "to strengthen, to encourage, to give strength." You're downcast, and along comes this strength and you are built up and encouraged. To receive comfort is to be buoyed up by God Himself.

There are at least four sources of that comfort. *First, the Lord Himself will come into your life* and, by His own Person, provide comfort. In 1 Samuel 30:6 we read that "David strengthened himself in the Lord his God." It was God who comforted him.

Second, the Scriptures come as a means of encouragement: Romans 15:4 tells us that "whatever was written in earlier times was written for our instruction, that through perseverance and the encouragement of the Scriptures we might have hope." How many times have you been hurting, physically, emotionally or spiritually, and you opened up the Word of God and the words ministered comfort and encouragement to you? I trust you can say this happened many times.

I have seen people in hospitals who were downcast and discouraged, and as I opened the Scriptures to them, the Word came as a bright light into their darkness; it lifted them out of their despondency and discouragement and the slough in which they were. Great is the comfort of Scriptures. How many times do we turn to the Psalms to buoy up our spirits? How many times do we turn to the Word of God when we discover nothing else will do? The Word of God ministers to us.

Third, the Holy Spirit is a source of comfort. The word *comfort* in the original Greek looks a little like the word for Holy Spirit which the Lord Jesus used when He said the Father would send "the Helper, the Holy Spirit" to earth (John 14:26). He's called the *paraclete*—one called alongside of, and the word *comfort* is from that same root. The ministry of the Holy Spirit is to stand alongside us, to comfort us. So when you have sorrow for your sin, or grieve over the loss of a loved one, the Holy Spirit comes alongside to lift and to comfort. He is the paraclete, the helper.

Fourth, God sends His own people to comfort you. In 2 Corinthians 7:6 we read that God comforted Paul through Titus when he came to him. Isn't it encouraging to know that another Christian may be sent by God to minister comfort to us when we need it? We need each other and I'm grateful for other Christians. I need you, you need me, we need each other for comfort. God has chosen people as ambassadors of comfort. Just recently I talked to a woman who had just lost her husband to a heart attack. This woman said that she had already been encouraged by Christians who had come alongside her. And what a help they were! You never know how important your fellow believers are until you've lost a loved one, how important they are when you are grieving over sin in your life; to have someone come alongside and be a means of spiritual encouragement to you, a means of God's comfort.

When does the comfort come? Sometimes it comes immediately. Jesus said to "come to Me . . . and I will give you rest" (Matt. 11:28), right now! If you didn't know Jesus Christ as your Saviour when you started this book and you don't know Him now, you could, by an act of personal faith, receive Him into your life and immediately become a child of the King. That can happen now. Today—"Now is the 'day of salvation' " (2 Cor. 6:2). Don't delay. That's instant comfort of God for those who mourn over their sin. Initially, it brings salvation, but it also continues throughout our lives with God, in our fellowship with Him. As we mourn for sin and confess it, God cleanses and restores us and we are comforted.

Sometimes comfort will be in the future. Remember Paul's words, "The sufferings of this present time are not worthy to be compared with the glory that is to be revealed to us" (Rom. 8:18)? You know what he's saying? You're going to go through those tough times, and you're going to feel the bumps of life, and you're going to be torn in your spirit, and you're going to be downcast, and you're going to feel empty and alone, and you're going to hurt; but Paul says: "Listen, the day is coming when all of this will pale into insignificance in the glory of the resurrected Christ which is your inheritance, and it will be worth it all." Count on it. "Weeping may last for the night, but a shout of joy comes in the morning" (Ps. 30:5). Sometimes that night is very long, but morning will come.

One of the dear ladies in our church died of a heart attack. While I was with her on the Monday night before she died on Tuesday she held my hand, gripping it very tightly, and said, "You're not going to forget me, are you?" I said, "Oh no, I'm not going to forget you." She said, "I won't forget you! We need each other." Then she said, "You know, I'd like to go home, I feel too good to be here. I want to go home!" Now, she prophesied something beyond what she had intended, perhaps, for she went home the next day. The sufferings of Monday "are not worthy to be compared to the glory" of Tuesday. And all you go through, all the tests and trials you may experience, are not worthy to be compared with the comfort that is eternal, purchased because Christ is our resurrected Lord. He triumphed, and that's our comfort. I can stand at a graveside with great confidence, if the person has trusted Christ. No question in my mind, his comfort has already come. The comfort for those who grieve is yet future if they're in Christ.

The Challenge to Your Life

Today, you can take that last part of this chapter and say, "Lord, today I sense my sin, I'm sorry for my sin, I grieve within regarding my sin, and today I want your cleansing." You're a Christian already, but sin has deprived you of fellowship and joy with the Lord. You don't feel good about your life—oh, you're a Christian, but that's about it. Right now you can say, "Lord, today I confess it, I grieve over it."

"Blessed are those who mourn for they shall be comforted." If you don't know Christ, your prayer should be, "Lord, I acknowledge my need, I confess you as my Saviour," and to you will come immediately the comfort of salvation. Peter, just before the cross, denied his Lord. Then he went out and wept bitterly; he mourned because of sin. This same sinful, selfish, defeated Peter experienced great joy when, later on, the risen Lord took that downcast Peter and lifted him, and gave him joy in the morning.

For Further Study

1. Explain how it is possible to be happy when you are mourning. Have you ever experienced this paradox? Explain.

2. How important is it to mourn over personal loss? personal sin?

3. What things prevent us from mourning over personal sin?

4. Make a list of all the places you currently turn to when you need comfort for personal sin. List them in order of their importance to you. Now, in light of the information from this chapter, should any source of comfort change? Would the order change? Why or why not?

CHAPTER FOUR

God's Gentle People

Matthew 5:5

It has been my privilege, over the past 20 years, to unite hundreds of couples in marriage, to see them come together and begin their lives, to sanctify themselves before God's people. Before that event occurs, I usually spend three or four sessions counseling with a couple. These are interesting times, perhaps more important in some respects than the service itself, as we think together about their lives as husband and wife.

As I reflect back on almost 20 years of marrying couples, I don't remember a single time when I asked the questions, "What do you love about her," or, "What do you love about him," that I've ever had one of them say, "I love him because he's meek." Never. Yet Jesus said, "Blessed are the gentle [meek], for they shall inherit the earth" (Matt. 5:5). The reason for this is that the world isn't very impressed with meekness.

Meekness—Who Wants It?

Who wants to be meek? "Meekness" immediately conjures up a picture of a weak, anemic, effeminate "sissy." It conjures up someone who is mousy, a Casper Milktoast who just appears and then slides back into the shadows. Someone you can stomp on. The kind of person, as one commentator puts it, who is like a subdued puppy crawling into his master's presence, whipped and beaten.

Who wants to be meek? Coaches don't like meek ballplayers. I've never yet heard a major-league coach say, "The thing that makes him a great ballplayer is that he's meek." They like the Pete Rose type, Mr. Hustle—kick dirt in the face of the second baseman; slide on his belly into third. Tough, hustle, aggressive—but meek? Never. Who wants a meek employee? How would you like to own a real-estate firm and have meek real-estate salesmen? You wouldn't make much money.

I guess husbands aren't necessarily impressed with looking for a meek wife. And certainly wives don't run around looking for a meek man to marry, unless they've got a pathological need for one. By and large, the meek aren't impressive to employers, to coaches, to wives, to husbands—who needs them? Who wants to be meek? Well, the Christian should. That's why the Word of God put it there. Evidently, there's something about meekness that we need.

Colleen Townsend Evans in her book on the Beatitudes, *A New Joy*, says, "I have a problem with this Beatitude. Frankly, I've never cared for it. Usually I pass over it quickly and try to ignore it. . . . Jesus—gentle, yes, but certainly not meek." But then she says something that we need to hear. "Jesus apparently thought it was important."[1] And therefore, we need to think it's important.

"Blessed are the gentle; blessed are the meek."

Meekness—Who Understands It?

Maybe our problem is definition. Who understands it? Well, *King James Version* translates it "meek"; *New American Standard Bible* gives us a little different flavor and calls it "gentle." We need to do some redefining; we need to correct our image, because if Jesus thought it was important, we ought to shift our thinking so that it becomes important to us too.

Let me give you some clues as to its meaning.

First, the Greeks thought it was important. The word here in Matthew 5:5 is *pràus,* and the Greeks had a number of ways of dealing with *pràus.* Aristotle always defined *virtue, or pràus* as the "mean between extremes." And when Aristotle defined meek, *pràus,* he said it is that person who is not excessively angry, always flying off the handle, nor is he the one who doesn't know how to be angry. A meek person is the one who is angry at the right time, in the right place, with the right people, and knows how to quit at the right time. Did you ever think of angry and meek together? That's its background.

A person who is meek, according to the original use of this word among Greek philosophers, is a person who is angry at the right time, at the right place, for the right reasons, with the right people, and knows how to quit at the right time. Do you know who is meek? Jesus. He wasn't angry when they spit on Him, He wasn't angry when they ridiculed Him, He wasn't angry when they challenged Him—He was angry at the right time, in the right place, with the right people; He knew to quit at the right time. He was angry when righteousness was at stake—He was angry with the Pharisees, because He was meek. He was angry at the disciples when they kept children from Him, because He was meek. *Meekness is being angry at the right time.*

A second way the Greeks defined the word was when it was used to refer to taming an animal. Here you have this ferocious animal who, all of a sudden, becomes domesticated. And the word here means "power under control." A meek person, from that connotation, is one who has power, who has strength, but is controlled and channels his power usefully rather than being destructive. It is not a person who gives up all his strength and power and ability; it is one who is domesticated and controlled. Meek was used in such a way as to be healing and helpful and positive. *Meekness is strength; it is power under control.*

The Old Testament also has a way of defining *meek*. Now you may, as you read the Beatitudes, get the impression that the Beatitudes were original with Jesus, and that's true with one exception: This one is not. If you'll turn back to Psalm 37 you'll discover that Jesus took this Beatitude from the psalmist David. He took it out of the Old Testament and incorporated it into the new life, for people within the Kingdom. Psalm 37:11 says: "But the humble will inherit the land." Or if you have the King James, it says "But the meek shall inherit the earth."

Who, then, are the meek who inherit the earth? In Psalm, 37:3, David says to "trust in the Lord." Verse 4: "Delight yourself in the Lord." Verse 5: "Commit your way to the Lord." Verse 7: "Rest in the Lord." Then he goes on to say, "The humble [or meek] shall inherit the earth." Who are they? They are people who bow to and are subservient to, and who depend upon and turn their will over and yield in obedience to, the Lord Himself. They commit their way to Him, they trust in Him, they rest in Him.

So, according to the biblical usage of that word, a meek person is one who has yielded himself and is obedient and trusts in his Lord.

The Old Testament tells us that Moses was the meekest of all men. That may not strike a responsive chord in you if you consider the popular definition of the word. You remember Moses coming down the mountain with the plates and when he discovered that the

Israelites had made a golden calf, he got *angry*! Remember their excuse? "We threw in the gold and out came this calf!" Talk about an excuse. Kids make up some pretty good ones, but never any better than Moses' people at that time. So Moses was angry; yet the Bible calls him the meekest of all men.

Numbers 12:3 refers to Moses as the meekest of all men. And this is what led to the description: Moses married a Cushite woman. Now a Cushite was a Black. And Moses married this black woman. There was nothing wrong with his marrying a black woman at this point—later on there were some legislations against marrying outside of Israel—but there was nothing wrong with it at the time Moses married this woman. However, Miriam his sister and his brother Aaron had a fit. They got all upset, and their racial prejudice came to the fore. They criticized him, they ridiculed him, but Moses didn't say a word.

So God came and held a conference with Moses, Aaron, and Miriam, and He rebuked them for criticizing Moses' marriage. This is one of those Old Testament passages that rebukes all racial pride. Because she opposed a black-white marriage, God struck Miriam with leprosy. One of the commentators said it's as if God were saying, "Alright, Miriam, you think white is best of all, you think that black is not beautiful—alright, have more of the white: here's leprosy. Have it fully."

What did Moses do during this whole thing? Never once did he talk back to Aaron or Miriam. Never once did he complain about the ridicule he took. Since he allowed himself to rest in the judgment of His God, and was subservient to the Lord, the Bible calls him "meek." Moses said, "If it's right, I'll be vindicated. If it isn't, then I'll stand judgment." He rested in the Lord. He trusted, committed his way to the Lord. A meek man is one who *yields his way in trust to the Lord* and lets the Lord settle the accounts.

The New Testament, however, takes the word meek and carries it further. Let's review the Beatitudes as we've covered them so far. "Blessed are the poor in spirit": The one who is poor in spirit is he who is bankrupt spiritually, the one who says, "Really, I have nothing to commend myself to God."

The next step is the next Beatitude: "Blessed are those who mourn." This Beatitude describes the one who is willing to repent of sin and grieves over it. He goes through great travail of spirit and soul. Blessed is that kind of a person who allows himself to travail over his sinful condition, who goes through sorrow, and is not afraid of tears.

Now, one step further, "Blessed are those who are meek." Not only am I bankrupt spiritually and greatly sorry for my sin, but when other people criticize me I don't answer back. Now it comes into the public market-place, for meekness is always a social grace that relates itself to others. When others say, "You know, you really are out of line," a meek or gentle person accepts it without reaction. A meek person in this context is a non-defensive person.

Martyn Lloyd-Jones, in a beautiful sermon, describes a meek person in this way: As God works in the heart of a person, that individual "is amazed that God and man can think of him as well as they do and treat him as well as they do."[2] Undefensive, regardless of what people say, he or she does not respond to it.

John Stott, the Anglican clergyman, speaks about a confession their churches make in their services which includes the line about being a "miserable sinner." He says, "It causes me no great problem. I can take it in my stride. But let somebody else come up to me after church and call me a miserable sinner, and I want to punch him in the nose."[3] It's one thing for us to say it; it's tough for someone else to say it. And a meek person is one who not only says it about his own life but allows others to say it without defending himself. He rests his case before God; he doesn't care what people say. That's power under control. That's being non-defensive. He is one who is essentially a tamed animal—who has power but has it under control; he rests his case in God.

When you begin to look at it in this light, "gentle" or "meek" is strength; nothing weak about that characteristic at all.

Meekness—Who Has It?

How do you know when you have meekness? Following are five questions that you can answer that will help you discover if you are truly a meek person. Have your wife or husband or a friend grade your answers and help you determine if you are meek or gentle.

1. *What is my attitude toward God's Word?* In James 1:21 it says we are to "in humility receive the word." How do you respond when God's Word addresses you? You are meek if you allow it to speak and you respond favorably to it. If you reject it, if you react against it, you're not meek yet. You are to receive His Word with meekness.

2. *What is my attitude toward a brother who sins?* How do you act when a brother or sister in Christ sins? Do you have a little delight in it? Think about it. When a star falls, do you feel a perverse sense of "I didn't think he was so good." It's kind of neat to discover weakness. That's the natural heart; that's not the redeemed, spiritual heart at all. You know what the Word of God says? Galatians 6:1—"Restore such a one in a spirit of gentleness."

How do you handle a brother or a sister who has fallen? In a spirit of meekness, knowing that it could be you? Do you go in tenderness and with a commitment to God, in a way that says, "I come to you. I care. Let's move in healing and health and restoration"? Restore such a one in a spirit of meekness. Are you meek? How do you respond to a brother who falls?

3. *What's your attitude toward a division in a church?*
When a church chooses up sides and comes into conflict,
how do you respond to that? Churches do this. Some of
you have been through it. Ephesians 4:2 and following
says, "With all humility and gentleness . . . preserve the
unity of the Spirit in the bond of peace." How do we
handle division in the church? A truly meek person seeks
humbly, gently, with power under control, to bring
about unity and oneness.

4. *What is my attitude toward those who disagree with
me?* When someone disagrees with you, how do you
respond? "Put up your dukes?" An eye for an eye, a
tooth for a tooth? Whop! And then give them the Four
Spiritual Laws? How do you handle disagreement?
Scripture reminds us, "With gentleness correcting those
who are in opposition" (2 Tim. 2:25). Not trying to
overwhelm and outmaneuver and aggressively stomp
them, but in meekness dealing with those who oppose.

5. *What is my attitude toward the unsaved?* What do
you think about them? Are you out to slay them with
gospel bombs? Are you out to overwhelm them with all
the wisdom you have because you're a Christian? How
do you handle the non-Christian? First Peter 3:15: Be
"ready to make a defense to every one who asks you to
give an account for the hope that is in you, yet with
gentleness and reverence." How you handle these situations will help you to discover if you are meek.

We have to pay the price for meekness. When do you inherit something? When someone dies. You inherit because a loved one or a friend dies and bequeaths it to you. Do you know how you inherit meekness? When someone dies—you! You die. That's how you inherit meekness. When "you have died with Christ" (Col. 2:20), have taken yourself off the throne not because you're weak but because that animal power is now under control, then you inherit meekness. Jesus said, "Come to Me, . . . learn from Me, for I am gentle and humble in heart" (Matt. 11:28,29). We're crucified with Him, and we accept His meekness.

Also, we have to yield to the Holy Spirit at this point. In Galatians 5:22,23 Paul names the fruit of the Spirit and one characteristic is gentleness. There's that word: meekness, gentleness. It is nothing I can build up; I can't construct meekness, I can't all of a sudden become instantly meek. It's a fruit of the Holy Spirit.

Meekness—What Does It Get You?

"Blessed are the gentle, for they shall inherit the earth." What is the inheritance that the gentle get? What does this mean? Well, it certainly doesn't mean that when you become gentle you will have larger real-estate holdings. You will not suddenly possess a much larger estate, live in a mansion instead of a tract house, lay claim to hundreds of acres. That doesn't come by being gentle. In fact, by the world's standards, that's the last way to get it.

You know what you inherit when you inherit the earth? You are at peace with your world, you are content, you are at rest. Paul put it this way: "I know how to get along with humble means, and I also know how to live in prosperity. . . . I can do all things through Him who strengthens me" (Phil. 4:12,13). I am His, I am at peace with my world, I have a contentment. I can move into this world that belongs to God, and I belong to Him and I am an heir of God and a joint heir with Christ (see Rom. 8:16,17). I can rest in contentment right now in my world. I'm at peace.

But there is also a future inheritance. In 2 Timothy 2:12 we are told we shall reign with Christ. There will be a new heaven and a new earth, and as heirs of God and joint heirs with Christ, the people of God will literally inherit the earth. It is ours. I don't care what your holdings are today; in Christ it will be better yet. And today you can know contentment and be at peace in your world, and have the assurance that God will provide eternally and abundantly. This is the blessing that comes to those who are gentle.

The Challenge to Your Life

How's your attitude? When do you get angry? At the right time, with the right people, for the right length of time? Are you a domesticated animal, or are you still wild and untamed?

God doesn't want to come into your life and squash you, He wants to channel you. He doesn't want to put you down, He wants to release you in a way that is positive and healing and healthy. You cannot for a moment look at the life of David and say, "There was a weak man." When he was in that cave he had Saul where he wanted him, he could have slain him; instead he cut off part of Saul's coat. That's power under control.

A gentle person, a domesticated child of God, rests his case with God. He has that power but it's under control. For my life I'd like more of that—how about you?

For just a few moments, quietly reflect on this attitude. Then maybe the response that needs to come from your heart today is, "Lord, too much of self, not enough of you. If I'm to inherit, I've got to die to self." God won't put you down; He will enable you to become a person of strength and courage and conviction, but it will be channeled.

That's the fruit of the Spirit: "Blessed are the gentle."

For Further Study

1. How do you think maintaining meekness might be different for a young adult than for a senior adult?

2. When is it difficult to maintain meekness in a job situation?

3. Why do you think it is difficult to be meek as a husband? As a wife?

Notes

1. Colleen Townsend Evans, *A New Joy* (Old Tappan, NJ: Fleming H. Revell, Co., 1973), p. 43.
2. D. Martyn Lloyd-Jones, *Studies in the Sermon on the Mount* (Grand Rapids: Wm. B. Eerdmans Publishing Co., 1977), p. 69.
3. John R.W. Stott, *Christian Counter-Culture* (Downers Grove, IL: Inter-Varsity Press, 1978), p. 43.

CHAPTER FIVE

Guaranteed Satisfaction

Matthew 5:6

I've picked up a nasty habit—it's called "eating." And quite frankly, I like it. I can sit in my study and fantasize over food and begin to salivate. I enjoy the smell of food. I can drive down the freeway and smell a bakery five miles away. I love the taste of food. Some of you, I'm sure, are of the same set.

Now eating is one habit you need—you should learn to manage it better, but you need food. It's basic to all of life. You need an appetite; without one you're dead. Without an appetite you have no vitality, you have no health. When it goes, you go. That applies to our spiritual appetites as well as our physical. "Blessed are those who hunger and thirst for righteousness, for they shall be satisfied" (Matt. 5:6).

An Appetite Is Basic to Life
In the natural realm, we don't simply *want* food and

drink, we *must* have food and drink. Food and drink are not luxuries. Maybe the extent to which we enjoy them is a luxury; but at rock bottom, we must have food and water to sustain ourselves, or we perish. One thing that has racked nations throughout history is the problem of famine. It was famine that sent Joseph's brothers to Egypt, their stomachs craving something they were not getting in their homeland. Across Europe there has been famine. In 879, 1016, 1162, thousands and thousands craved food and could not have it, and they died. Even during the sophisticated nineteenth century, with all its advances, there was famine in countries like Russia, China, Ireland and India, leaving thousands dead. Today in India the havoc of malnutrition still racks that great nation. Food is not a luxury. Bread and water, food and drink are essential, basic ingredients of physical sustenance.

Jesus takes that theme and carries it one step further by saying, "Blessed are those who hunger and thirst after righteousness, for they shall be satisfied." He is saying, "Just as food and water are basic to the physical life, righteousness is basic to the spiritual. What is true in our physical bodies is also true spiritually." And unless there is a craving after righteousness, you will perish spiritually. It is basic—it is not a luxury. To hunger and thirst after righteousness is the only way to be sustained; it is the only way to survive; it is the only way to avoid perishing. What is this *righteousness* we are to hunger and thirst for?

Righteousness is goodness, it is holiness, it is the gift of God to His people. Billy Graham states it in this fashion: "It is God's sharing His nature with us. We become partakers of divine life." When I hunger and thirst, God gives me of His own life. Righteousness is not something that comes from within—it is a gift from God. It is a gift to those who hunger and thirst after it, who seek it from God. It is God's life imparted to me, imparted to you. It is God's life given to those who hunger and thirst.

Righteousness, scripturally, takes on three dimensions: (1) Legal—justification; (2) moral—sanctification; (3) eternal—glorification.

God's righteousness has a legal dimension—justification. The Bible talks about our being justified before God: "Therefore having been justified by faith, we have peace with God through our Lord Jesus Christ" (Rom. 5:1). When we, by faith, receive Christ, He gives us His life and we stand upon the foundation of Christ; we are justified, we become righteous in God's eyes. We no longer are under the penalty of sin.

I don't care what you've done or how much you've done of it—all your sin is covered, it's past. Calvary covers it all. By faith we received the righteousness of God and we stand legally justified before Him. We are acquitted. That is legal righteousness. If you're a Christian, if you're born again, if you're saved, "you have been saved through faith; . . . it is the gift of God" (Eph. 2:8).

God's righteousness has a moral dimension—sanctification. Now, sanctification isn't like justification. At some point in your life you trusted Christ and your life was changed; you can point to that time in your life. You know when you were born again. You became a new creature in Christ Jesus. That was legal righteousness. It was a one-time decision. But moral righteousness is perpetual; it is something dynamic, an on-going activity in your life. It is not static—you don't look back and say, "I was sanctified." You are being sanctified; you are in the process of "becoming." You are a "becomer," as Keith Miller puts it. You are in process.

Now, negatively, sanctification is a turning from sin, turning from those things that displease God. The closer you walk to the Lord, the more sensitive you are about what does and what doesn't satisfy Him. Positively, sanctification means that you are expressing more of the fruit of the Spirit—in your daily life, on the job, on the freeway, with your mate, with your children, with your parents, with whomever. More and more, as you are in this process of moral sanctification, you show more of Jesus Christ in you. When you hunger and thirst after it, He gives it to you day by day—more and more of His own person, more and more of His own nature: a perpetual growing relationship in Christ. That's moral righteousness.

God's righteousness also has an eternal dimension—glorification. Someday we will enter the presence of God and then, "the God of peace Himself will sanctify you entirely; . . . your spirit and soul and body . . . complete . . . at the coming of our Lord Jesus Christ" (1 Thess. 5:23). That means that in the day of His coming—the second return of our Lord—we will be made complete, total. That's when our righteousness becomes eternal and covers every part of us; even our bodies are then redeemed.

So when we are saved, we *are* made righteous, free of the penalty of sin; as we grow, we *are becoming* righteous, we are free of the power of sin; but someday, we *shall be* perfectly righteous, free of the very presence of sin. That's the righteousness He gives to those who hunger and thirst.

A Lost Appetite Is a Symptom of Sickness

Some people have lost their appetite. That's a tragedy. Have you ever known a child who lives life with gusto? He charges into his meals; he charges around the house; he runs hard; he plays hard; he eats heartily. Then all of a sudden this kid, who has been driving you crazy, begins to act the way you had been wishing he would. He becomes quiet and listless and terribly obedient. He doesn't want to eat. He just looks kind of glassy-eyed at the food. He loses his appetite. He gets sick. Then you feel bad.

A loss of appetite is one of the first symptoms of diminishing health. When I visit someone in the hospital I tend to ask the question, "How are you eating?" Sometimes the response is, "Oh, I'm really eating fine. The hospital food's good." Then I know the patient is on the mend. But, if the person responds, "Not so good. I just can't seem to eat," and he pushes the food away, you know something is not quite right yet. When health returns, so does appetite. People can lose their appetites spiritually under certain conditions. I've listed three of them.

First, nothing can spoil your appetite for God's righteousness like unconfessed sin. When you're living in unconfessed sin you have no craving after righteousness. Paul wrote to Timothy, "Demas, having loved this present world, has deserted me" (2 Tim. 4:10). A desire for this "present world"—and the *world* here represents its standards of morality, life and style—spoils your appetite for righteousness. Demas deserted Paul; he went his own way because he had lost his appetite for the things of God. That happens. Unconfessed sin has a way of crowding out the spiritual appetite so that you no longer hunger and thirst after righteousness and after the holiness of God.

Second, self-satisfaction will spoil your appetite for righteousness. Remember the church at Laodicea which Revelation speaks about? They thought they were so healthy, but God said, "You're sick and you don't know it" (see Rev. 3:14-18). Nothing is quite so tragic as a person who goes along as if he's doing well, and yet he's dying; or the person who thinks he's spiritually full, and he's starving. Self-satisfaction insulates us from an appetite for the things of God.

A third thing that spoils our appetite for righteousness is misunderstanding. Suppose you're at the office and decide to call your wife at home. During the conversation you casually ask, "What's for dinner tonight?" She responds, "Oh, we're going to have leftovers." Somehow your appetite goes right out the window. But if she says, "We're going to have French ragout" (which is actually made from leftover beef and gravy) your mouth begins to water. Our experience with leftovers doesn't trigger any excitement, any appetite. Some people react that way when they hear about someone who is "holy," or spiritual. They say, "Boy, I know people like that, and quite frankly I don't want it." Some people have no hunger for righteousness because it doesn't seem to be very satisfying. They see only the caricature of righteousness. There are several reasons for this misunderstanding.

A lot of people see *Pharisee righteousness.* In Jesus' day, people were turned off by the righteousness of the Pharisees. All they saw were shriveled lives of supercritical people. The Pharisees lived lives focused on externals—don't do this, don't do that—and paraded their brand of "righteousness" for everyone to see. Their life-style didn't make them very happy and didn't stimulate those around them to emulate it. Therefore, few people craved that kind of holiness. Holiness and being miserable were associated; they were one and the same in the people's eyes.

If the kind of righteousness you see in some Christians makes them miserable, you haven't seen the right thing yet. So, you may misunderstand righteousness. The right kind of righteousness is a liberating, life-giving vitality; the life of God in a person that frees him to really live! That's the kind of righteousness you will crave. But if you misunderstand it and see it only as a deterioration of the human experience, as something that is suffocating rather than liberating, you won't want it. A lot of people have lost their appetite because they don't want to hunger and thirst after a caricature of righteousness.

The second misunderstanding is caused by a *loss of individuality*. This quality was also exemplified by the Pharisees. They all looked and acted alike. You might as well have stamped them out with a cookie cutter, because they only had external righteousness. On the other hand, the apostles were 12 distinct individuals, each with his own personality and uniqueness, because they had the righteousness of God. The more Christlike you become, the more freed up you are to be the person God created. You don't lose your individuality—it is heightened.

Christ does not grind us all down to the lowest common denominator where we look alike, sound alike, and act alike. No, He takes us and fills us with His life and enables us to be the gifted persons we should be. You don't lose your individuality. So, if you lack an appetite for the things of God because you think it's going to flatten out your personality, you don't know what righteousness is all about. You are missing the color and fervor and vitality and poignancy which God intended you to have. For the righteousness of Christ makes you a new person in Him, with all the potential of the new man in Christ.

A Hearty Appetite Is a Promise of Health

Now, a hearty appetite usually indicates good health. The text goes on to say, "Blessed are those who hunger and thirst for righteousness, *for they shall be satisfied*" (Matt. 5:6, italics added). When you hunger and thirst after the righteousness of God, He says, "I will meet that need." When you see the sick child's appetite reviving and he begins to move around again, you say, "He's coming alive! Hang on! Nail things down. Put things on the top shelf. Health is back." And when we see a Christian craving after more of the holiness of God and the righteousness of Jesus Christ, that's a healthy sign. It's a sign of vitality.

When does satisfaction come? Satisfaction, filling, comes in three ways.

First, God fills us instantly. If you know that you have never walked into the newness of life, if you know that you are not a new creature in Christ Jesus, if you're carrying the burden of your sin, if you're shackled by it, if you feel the guilt of it and you've never known the transforming power of Jesus Christ, right now you could receive the righteousness of God. By an act of personal faith you can say, "Lord, I look at my life. I'm a sinner, I confess that. I'm sorry for it, I repent of it. I receive you as my Saviour. Come into my life." And He will! Instantly! God stands behind His promise. That promise has an eternal satisfaction guarantee, right now—the righteousness of God.

Second, God fills us progressively. When Jesus met with the multitudes He fed them physically (see Matt. 15:30-38; John 6:1-13). Remember what He said after that meal? "I am the bread of life; he who comes to Me shall not hunger, and he who believes in Me shall never thirst" (John 6:35). He was talking about spiritual filling. When you take of Him you are immediately satisfied. You will never again thirst after that *legal* righteousness, which is justification. But hunger and thirst will continue in your life, for, as in the other beatitudes, the condition of hungering and thirsting is progressive. Poverty of spirit is a continual recognition of bankruptcy; mourning for sin must be continuous; gentleness is a continuing spirit. All of these are continual, progressive. None of them is nailed down. None of them is past tense. They all continue. Hungering and thirsting after righteousness, that which we call *moral righteousness*, is something that will go on all your life.

Look back at yourself a year ago today. Where were

you as a person in Christ? Where are you this minute? Have you progressed spiritually? You should have. God's people ought to be people on the "grow." A people who are continually walking and experiencing His life. You will not be where you are today a year from now. God has more for you than you have already experienced. Count on it! He will continue to satisfy your hunger and thirst for righteousness.

Finally, God will fill us permanently. Someday the promise will be fulfilled, perfectly and absolutely. When we come into His presence we will be faultless, without spot, blameless. That's still to come. It isn't here yet. Until then, you will continue to hunger and thirst. You will finish one meal then go about your life and, late in the afternoon, hunger will return. And the more you hunger and thirst after God, the more you're satisfied, and the more you want. You kind of pick up a good habit. And, praise God, you can't overeat spiritually. You cannot have too much of God. The more you eat of His sustenance, the more you partake of His offering of Himself and His Word and His own righteousness, the more you want. *The more you want!*

The Challenge to Your Life
Part of our difficulty is that we hunger and thirst after happiness or we hunger and thirst after experience; and we never receive either one. You have to get the horse before the cart. When you hunger and thirst after God,

He will give you satisfaction; He will give you experience; He will give you joy. But happy and satisfied are we when we hunger and thirst for righteousness, for we will be filled, completely satisfied, full of joy.

For what do you hunger?

"Blessed are those who hunger and thirst for righteousness."

For Further Study

1. What is the difference between righteousness and legalism?

2. What are some reasons it might be difficult to hunger or thirst after righteousness in a marriage? In a family?

3. Look back at yourself a year ago today. Where were you as a person in Christ? Where are you right now? Have you progressed spiritually? What are your spiritual goals for this next year?

Note
1. Keith Miller, *The Becomers* (Waco, TX: Word Books, 1973).

CHAPTER SIX

It's God-Like to Be Merciful

Matthew 5:7

"Blessed are the merciful, for they shall receive mercy" (Matt. 5:7). In this Beatitude, Jesus takes the fluttering pulse of the Christian church and diagnoses one of our problems. The Great Physician, in terse words, lays His hand upon one of our basic sicknesses— our utter selfishness.

Look how often you use personal possessive pronouns: *My* car; *my* house; *my* job; *my* church; *my* denomination; *my* problem; *my* pressures; *my* headache; *my* boss. My, my, my—that's really the nature of life. If you ask someone to try out a pen, what does he write? His name! He doesn't write someone else's name.

We're very caught up in things of "me," things that are "mine." And in this Beatitude, Jesus takes us beyond that and says we are to be a channel through which His mercy and His love reach out to others. We have been made the grand recipients of His mercy, and we now are to be clear channels through which His mercy is experienced in others' lives. "Blessed are the merciful, for they shall receive mercy."

Mercy Is a Many-Splendored Attribute

John Stott says, "Mercy is compassion for people in need." But you can't simply leave it there. Compassion is an attitude of the heart, something internal. The word *mercy* takes us beyond compassion; mercy is an internalized feeling that reaches out to actually do something. It is pity plus action. It is compassion plus an attempt to resolve and to care for that hurt, that suffering—to relieve it.

Mercy is an attribute of God. When we're merciful, we are God-like. The Scriptures tell us again and again, "God is merciful." The theologians tell us that there are two types of attributes of God: (1) *absolute attributes* and (2) *relative attributes*.

Absolute attributes are things about God that are true regardless; they are absolute truth—God is love, God is holy, God is truth. These attributes are irrespective of His relationship to us. They are *absolute attributes* of God.

Relative attributes of God come into play when man comes into being. From the creation of man we have the expression of God's relative attributes. They have meaning only in relation to us. What does that mean? It means simply that His absolute attribute of love, when expressed to us relatively, is mercy. Love is absolute, mercy is the expression of that love to us; mercy and grace. God is truth; that's absolute. The relative attribute is that He is faithful. His faithfulness is an expression of His truth. He is holy; that's an absolute attribute. God is holy, and it's expressed in His justice toward us.

God's mercy is the expression of His love toward us. Notice how often in Scripture mercy and grace are tied together? Almost like twins, in fact. The reason they are linked together is that grace is in relation to man's sin; mercy is in relation to man's misery, which may be the result of sin. Grace for our sin, mercy for our suffering and for our misery. Grace comes along to pardon; mercy comes along to heal. Grace cleanses and reinstates; mercy relieves, helps, cures. Out of the grace of God we have been saved. Out of His mercy we have been helped and we have been healed and cared for. His grace and His mercy are both expressions of His love toward us.

Mercy is basically an attitude; it arises out of the heart. Mercy finds expression externally, but it arises out of the heart. Christianity is always of the heart. The Pharisees had an external righteousness: We did this, we did that, we did these deeds. Jesus comes along and says, "But I say unto you, what about your heart? You say you have done these things, but is your heart that way?" The gospel of our Christ is the gospel of the heart, an internal thing. And mercy comes out of the heart, an expression of a merciful heart. When God changes our hearts, it's an internal action, a miracle of God's grace. He comes in and makes us merciful within, and then, of course, it is expressed in external acts of pity.

Mercy is a chain of four links: pain, power, pity, participation.

Link one—pain. First of all there has to be a need or mercy is irrelevant. Who needs mercy if you don't have a need? You don't go around expressing mercy to people who have no need. You don't help ladies across the street who don't want to cross the street, even if you are a Boy Scout! If a person doesn't have a need, there's no need for mercy. Mercy always arises out of some hurt, some brokenness, some pain that has come physically or emotionally or spiritually—there is a brokenness that gives rise to mercy. You always start there.

Link two—power. You and I have to have the power to do something about the pain. One writer says, "Unless we have the power to inflict further pain, we don't have the power to inflict healing." That is to say there comes, in the response of pain, an opportunity to do something either helpful or hurtful, and you have that ability. And unless you have that ability, you really have not responded in mercy. Let me illustrate this by two biblical stories. Do you remember Joseph? He's in Egypt, and he has power. His brothers come to him and they need food. Now Joseph has the power to inflict further pain upon them and deny them food. He has that power. He chooses rather to alleviate their pain and he uses his power constructively. He feeds them.

Remember when David encountered Saul in a cave? David had the power to kill Saul, to do him in with a sword, to inflict great pain to his body; he had that power. He chose rather to show him kindness and mercy. So you have the power to inflict further pain or to heal. Mercy uses the power to heal.

Link three—pity. You see the need. You see someone who has gone through a great time of crisis, and they're broken, and you know it. Your heart goes out to them. That's pity. The responsiveness of Christ within us is one of mercy. He is mercy-giving and His people, when they are Christ-like, are merciful and they reach out in pity and compassion. Their own hearts cry out; they hurt with the hurting.

Link four—participation. This is doing something in terms of action and activity in an attempt to alleviate pain, to alleviate hurt, and to bind together the brokenness. And so we have four links of mercy: when we see pain we respond with our power, then our pity, and finally with participation. Pain plus power plus pity plus participation equals mercy. Short of that, mercy is not full. It is not complete.

Mercy Is a Much-Needed Ministry

Who needs mercy? Every one of us. There will come times when we'll need it more than others. There will come times when we can extend mercy and there will come times when we will need mercy. I've needed it, and you've needed it, and you may need it right now. There are four conditions which require mercy.

The lost need mercy. There is nothing so miserable as a person who is wallowing in his sin, is lost and away from God, alienated from God. The lost man or woman who knows it and is broken in it needs you to go to him with that merciful word that Jesus Christ receives sinful men. That's a word of mercy, and that's a healthy word—people getting their lives put together. They're hurting spiritually, and they need to be bound up by a word of mercy in salvation.

A second group that needs mercy is the clobbered. I couldn't think of a better word for it. People who've just been busted, been shattered and scattered in their experience, whose whole lives are shattered. They've been hit upon the anvil of human experience and they're broken. They've been clobbered—there's no other word for it. Folks who've just gone through a divorce, who have just had a loved one wrenched out of their grip, who are hanging with breaking fingernails onto a precipice because of some great accident or crisis in their lives, who are reaching out because they've been broken; they've been clobbered.

That happened to a man who was taking a trip from Jericho to Jerusalem. He had to travel along a rocky road, a very treacherous road, a road that you really didn't travel alone if you had a choice. On his way he was assaulted and beaten and left to die. He was clobbered.

Along came a priest who looked at him, had a little

pity, perhaps, in his heart, but he didn't participate—no mercy. He had the power to do something. There was the pain, and maybe he had a little pity, but he didn't show mercy.

A Levite did the same thing. Too busy. I don't know what they were on their way to do: sermon preparation, pastor's meeting; they had no time for mercy. They just looked and went on.

Then along came a Samaritan—and what did he do? He extended mercy. He got off his donkey and extended mercy to a man who was clobbered and near death (see Luke 10:30-35). Sometimes those around us have been hit just like that. They are hurting; maybe you can't experience that, maybe you can't understand that unless you've been there, but they're hurting. It's critical.

Another group that need mercy are those who are aching. If the clobbered could be described as critical, I would say that the aching are chronic. The aching are those who have an ongoing battle with loneliness, who would like to be sharing their lives with others but feel like they're an island when they'd love to be a peninsula. They feel alone, all alone. They can join fifty thousand at a big ballgame and cheer and yet they know, regardless of how many are with them, they're still alone. Maybe you go to church on Sunday morning and you're with hundreds of others and yet you feel, "I'm all alone." You're aching. What do the lonely need? Mercy!

The aching are also those who are discouraged. Someone who is discouraged needs a person to come up alongside them and offer an encouraging word. Someone to come alongside, as does the Spirit the *Paraclete*.

The aching are also those who are in sickrooms. They need someone to come alongside of their bed and extend their life, expand their room and make it a larger place, a temple where they meet God through you. Those who are aching need mercy.

The last group that needs mercy is those who are guilty. There are folks who are carrying great guilt—maybe you're one of them. You've offended another and it bothers you. You carry it like a heavy burden. It goads you, it dogs your steps—you feel very guilty. You need someone to come alongside and lift that guilt and say, "You've disappointed me, you may have hurt me, but I want you to know I forgive you." What do the guilty need? They need that word of forgiveness.

Remember Jesus with Peter? Peter was so gifted, so adept at doing things when he was on target; yet so incompetent at certain times. So much like some of us. Like me. He denied his Lord; he cursed. Jesus went to the cross. Peter was left, a man with a heavy burden. Guilty! You know what Jesus did on Easter morning? He went to Peter. He put His arm around that big, brawny shoulder. Peter's leathery face was downcast, but all of a sudden it began to lighten as Jesus said, "Peter, I love you. I extend to you My care, My mercy. I love you. Rise up, serve Me again." That's a word of mercy to the guilty.

Mercy Is a Twice-Blessed Grace

"Blessed are the merciful, for they shall receive mercy." You readers of Shakespeare, remember Portia's speech in the *Merchant of Venice*? "The quality of mercy is twice-blessed; it blesses him that gives, and him that takes." How true! When you extend mercy you receive it.

It's not that you show mercy just to get mercy; that's not it. You don't give to get. That's not the spirit of mercy. But it just happens that the merciful become the obvious recipients of mercy. If mercy has to be earned, it shoots holes in all the theology of grace and brings into disrepute all of those things that are associated with grace and mercy. Mercy is unmerited. The merciful are a humble people, a repentant people, and they receive mercy. The merciful see what sin has done in people's lives and rather than judging them, they provide mercy. Haven't you reached out at times, maybe not enough, but when you've done it you've discovered that not only did you give, but God gave to you? Sure you have. If you haven't, I can promise it—it's part of God's Word; it's a promise of our Christ.

The Challenge to Your Life

Mercy surrounds us. Have you ever thought about it? Our past, our future, our present. We can look back on our life and say, "Surely goodness and mercy have followed me all the days of my life." They have! That's past. We can look to the future and say, as Jude 21 says,

We are "waiting anxiously for the mercy of our Lord Jesus Christ to eternal life." That's completion with Him. That's future.

But today is mercy-filled as well. Listen to the word that comes to us out of Lamentations 3:22: "It is of the Lord's mercies that we are not consumed, because his compassions fail not. They are new every morning; great is thy faithfulness" (*KJV*). You can look back and say, "Great are His mercies." You can look forward and say, "His mercy is to be extended." You can look at today and say, "His mercies are new every day." You and I have been the grateful benefactors of so much mercy. Praise God for that.

But now will you join me in saying, "Lord, I have received of your mercy, I have received mercy from others; help me now to be a channel through whom your mercy can flow." This is the outflowing Beatitude. Up to now it's all been, "This is *my* spirit: *I* am broken, *I* am spiritually bankrupt—that's what it means to be poor in spirit—*I* mourn, *I* am meek—which is my response to people." Now you can reach out. "Blessed are the merciful."

Do you know someone who's lonely that you ought to visit? Do you know somebody who is sick that needs a call or a card, or maybe a visit? Do you know somebody who has recently been fractured and is hurting through a divorce, through a death? Let the Lord jog your memory. If the Spirit of God assigns it, won't you do it? Maybe you need to say, "Lord, I want to show what

you've shown to me; help me to reach out in mercy."
"Blessed are the merciful."

For Further Study

1. What are some reasons you may find it difficult to show mercy with your children? Why is it important to let our children show mercy to us as parents?

2. Why is it important that we continue to show mercy as well as receive it throughout our lives?

3. Discuss which of the four conditions that require mercy seems most appropriate for your personal ministry.

CHAPTER SEVEN

Do You Have Integrity?

Matthew 5:8

Our sight is a very special treasure, but it's something we take for granted until we see someone walking down the street, tapping his way along sightlessly. When I see a blind person, all of a sudden I'm brought up short. My heart goes out to him. It hurts to see someone moving through life with eyes that don't see. They miss so much (or so we think).

The Scripture reminds us that the same thing happens spiritually. People who are not pure in heart tap their way through life spiritually, and never see God. The Beatitude tells us, "Blessed are the pure in heart, for *they* shall see God" (Matt. 5:8).

Christianity Focuses on the Primacy of the Heart

Christianity focuses on the heart; the center of our personality is the heart. In Bible language the heart is the very core of our being. It includes our minds, our will and our emotions. Someone has called it the "control center" of the person. Jesus' whole problem with the Pharisees was that they had focused upon externals. He brought them back and said "No, it's not just what you do, and how you act—the externals of life—I'm concerned about the heart, the very control center of your being. What's going on within? What's going on at the heart of your being?"

Proverbs 4:23 reminds us, "Watch over your heart with all diligence, for from it flow the springs of life." The essence of a man or a woman is what's within; all that you are is an expression of who you are at the heart of your being. When your heart is right, your life is right; when your heart is bad, this control center leads the rest of your being, your life, astray.

The heart is the source of all our troubles. Someone said that you can blame people or you can blame circumstances, but the Bible blames the heart. Jeremiah says that "the heart is more deceitful than all else and is desperately sick" (17:9). By nature, our heart is deceitful; it is full of all that which is wicked. Matthew 15 talks about all the things that flow from the heart; it's the source of all our troubles. We try to blame other things, "It's my lousy environment!" We may blame other people, "You know, others create all my problems. The reason I'm this way is because I live with these folks, or I work with that person." We may blame our environment, but the Lord says, "It's your heart." About the time we're ready to blame our environment, we remember man fell while he was in Paradise where the environment was perfect. It's the other way around: once our heart gets into it, we ruin the environment. The heart is the source of our trouble. We need a heart that is pure before God.

Christ Calls for Purity of Heart

What does it mean to be "pure in heart"? First of all, it means *inward purity*. The word *purity* has two meanings. The first means just plain "clean." We get the Greek word *cathartic* from this word. When a doctor works with you, he tries to do something cathartic, to cleanse, to purify your system of that which is giving you poor health. He can bring about that catharsis physically. The psychologist or the psychiatrist tries to bring catharsis emotionally, to cleanse you of anything that is impure in terms of emotional drives; any emotion that is fouling up your system. What Jesus calls us to is a life where the heart is purified before Him, a heart that has been cleansed spiritually.

David, as you know, became involved in deep sin. Listen to his prayer in Psalm 51—and it can apply to his sin or to the variety of sins that we may get involved in: "Behold, Thou dost desire truth in the innermost being, and in the hidden part Thou wilt make me know wisdom. Purify me with hyssop, and I shall be clean; wash me, and I shall be whiter than snow. Make me to hear joy and gladness; let the bones which Thou hast broken rejoice.

Hide Thy face from my sins, and blot out all my iniquities" (Ps. 51:6-9). Then David pleads, "Create in me a clean heart."

When Jesus says the pure in heart shall see God, He is saying that our heart needs to be purified and cleansed by God Himself. Cleansed of sin and impurity. It's just that simple—in statement, but not always in practice. Our hearts become clouded and fouled up with impure motives and impure desires and impurity of will, and God has to come along and purify our heart—cleanse it.

Does that say something to you today? Is your heart of that nature? God says we need inward purity. That's our personal relationship to self, and to our God.

But secondly "pure in heart" means sincerity. The word also means "unmixed." Kierkegaard said that purity of heart is "to will one thing." No deceit. Milk that has no added water in it is pure. Gold without dross is pure gold. Jesus is saying: "Look, get your heart right. Have integrity. When you say something, mean what you say."

I heard Dr. Carl Lundquist, the president of Bethel College and Seminary, a few years ago in San Diego. He reported that there is now a way for you to determine when a politician is lying by watching for certain signals. For example, if a politician rubs his hair a certain way, he's not lying. If he mops his brow, he's not lying either. But if he moves his lips . . . Well, politicians don't have a corner on lying. And there are some good politicians and there are some Christians without integrity. When we move our lips, do we speak truth? Is what we say without "forked tongue?"

To whom are we to be pure in heart? We are supposed to first be pure in heart *toward God.* I delight in David. As you read the Psalms, one of the things that is very striking is that when he was troubled he told God, "God, I'm troubled!" If he was discouraged he told it all to God. In the Scriptures we are reminded that the Lord heard David because he was always going before Him with his problems, his frustrations, his anger. He got mad at people, remember? "Lord, go out and stomp on them!" If he felt it, he told God. There was nothing hidden with David.

There are only two experiences in the life of David in the biblical record in which he was deceitful, and both got him into trouble. But the rest of life he was open; he poured out his life and said, "Here are my complaints, Lord." The Lord can deal with people who have integrity. God can handle your frustrations, your anger. Let Him have them. He can handle them. Share your complaints. Be open with your Lord.

Secondly, we have to be pure in heart with *other people,* not only with God. Now, this doesn't mean you share every feeling you've ever had about everybody. No, none of us is ready to handle that. But it does mean that there is a transparency about our experience, that there is an openness about us.

Remember the story of Nathanael? I like Nathanael.

I used to think he was one of the New Testament bad boys. Philip goes to him and says, "You've got to come and meet Jesus Christ." Remember Nathanael's comment? "Can any good thing come out of Nazareth?" I used to think, "Of all the bigots, Nathanael is numero uno!" Jesus meets Nathanael and what does He say? "Indeed, an Israelite in whom is no guile!" What was He saying? He is saying that Nathanael is single-minded: what he feels, he says. That's integrity. Your word is good. You don't play games, manipulating, moving in and out of roles; you don't wear a mask. The pure in heart are those who have integrity, whose word is good.

How can you learn to be "pure in heart"? There are four sources of help.

The first is the Word of God itself. "How can a young man keep his way pure? By keeping it according to Thy Word" (Ps. 119:9). "Thy Word I have treasured in my heart, that I may not sin against Thee" (Ps. 119:11). Have you noticed that if your life is blotched by sin and you get into the Word, there is a purifying effect? God's Word reveals our need to us and drives us back to confession. The Word does that.

Secondly, the Holy Spirit helps us become "pure in heart." Acts 15:8,9 remind us that God gave "them the Holy Spirit, just as He also did to us; . . . cleansing their hearts by faith." The ministry of the Holy Spirit is to come within and purify our hearts. That's one of His ministries. When you're a Christian He dwells in your heart. He is there to purify it. Have you ever been out when it was muddy, and your clothes got full of mud and dirt, and the wind blew everything askew? You know the only part of you that was still clean externally? Your eyes. Your eyes keep clear and bright because they are constantly being washed by the eyelids and those little fountains within. Everything else about you may be a mess, and you may need to shower, clothes and all, but your eyes keep clean because they are constantly being washed. In the same way the Holy Spirit works within us to continually purify us.

The blood of Christ helps us to be "pure in heart." "The blood of Jesus His Son cleanses us from all sin," we're told in 1 John 1:7, and that's what the Holy Spirit uses: the blood of Christ. That's what He applies to our sin.

And then lastly, *there is the blessed hope that makes us "pure in heart."* First John 3:3 reminds us that "every one who has this hope fixed on Him purifies himself, just as He is pure." Why is it that thinking about and hoping for His return will purify us? If you know you're having company, what happens in your house? Your house may look like Genesis 1:1, without form and void and darkness upon the face of the deep. Then you "breathe" on it, cleaning and straightening. When your guests walk in, they think your house always looks like that! The hope of company has a way of purifying and cleansing your house.

Well, when we have the blessed hope that the Lord

will return, we will by occupying till He comes. We're a people who are prepared so that when He comes, we are ready for Him. Pure hearts—He's coming again. I want to meet Him, and be prepared.

Gospel Promises a Vision of God

The promise in this sixth Beatitude is that "the pure in heart shall see God." Since nothing is higher than God Himself, the highest experience in all of life must be to see God. When do we see Him? We see Him now, revealed in what I call the four Cs of revelation.

First of all, we're going to see Him in creation. Psalm 19:1 reminds us that "the heavens are telling of the glory of God; and the firmament is declaring the work of His hands." Coming back from Wheaton some time ago, I stopped for a few hours in Colorado. I was taken to the airplane by a man by the name of Chuck. Chuck poured out his heart and shared with me what he'd gone through in the last five years. He'd lost two children, ages 11 and 18. He told me a shocking fact, and that is that of the parents who lose teenagers, three out of four get a divorce. The tragedy, rather than bringing them together, tears them apart.

Chuck belongs to an organization that is working to heal those situations. But as I drove to the airport with him, listening to him tell me about going through all of this, I felt the anguish of his soul. We drove by those beautiful, magnificent Colorado mountains. He looked up at them and said, "How can anybody look at that and not know there's a God?" I would have thought that he, having gone through what he has, would have his vision clouded, but it hasn't been. The heavens, the creation, reveals God's handiwork. Through the eyes of faith the believer sees the magnificent artistry of our God, His creation. And, at the bottom of the canvas it's signed, "God."

God is revealed also in circumstances. Psalm 23:4 says "Even though I walk through the valley of the shadow of death, I fear no evil; for Thou art with me." You move through situations that may tear you apart and you think the bottom has fallen out, the sun has been cut off, that you are in the valley of shadows. Yet even in the midst of those circumstances, God says "I am with you." We can see Him there.

I believe it was Dr. A. T. Pierson who first said "History is His story." God, through circumstances and through time, is working to accomplish His purposes, and we see Him. Many of us have watched doors open and doors shut in our lives, and have seen things come together in such a way that we know God is at work in our midst. Creation reveals Him, but so do our personal circumstances.

Christians reveal God. One of the thrilling things that God has allowed to happen is to let Himself be known through the Body of Christ, the church. Have you ever met Christians who revealed to you the very presence of our Lord? When you met them, you saw the Lord in them?

My professor back in seminary, Dr. Clarence Roddy, was overwhelmed when his son came to him and said, "Dad, when I see your face, I see the face of Christ." Jesus Christ is seen in His church. A number of people come flooding to my mind when I think about the reality of Christ in His redeemed people.

The fourth C where we see God now is in communion with Him. Martyn Lloyd-Jones puts it this way: "There is a seeing also in the sense of knowing Him, a sense of feeling He is near, and enjoying His presence."[1] In your walk with God, in your communion with Him, there is an opening of the eyes of faith where you meet Jesus Christ—you see Him. In personal worship, in personal communion, you walk in fellowship with Him. That's now.

Not only do we see Him now through the four Cs, we *will see Him someday.* Remember what 1 Corinthians 13:12 says? "Now we see in a mirror dimly." It's a description of an image reflected in the inadequate mirrors of the first century. They showed a fuzzy image of the one looking in them. The Word of God reminds us that we can only see in the mirror dimly right now, but someday we shall see Him "face to face." One of the privileges of the redeemed is that we shall know Him and shall be with Him and shall see Him and enjoy the vision of God throughout all eternity. That has to be the highest experience of all of life, to see Him and experience Him for all of eternity. "Blessed are the pure in heart, for they shall see God."

The Challenge to Your Life

It's fascinating to discover that when you begin to experience that purity of the heart (which is the cleansing of sin) and sincerity (which is a denial of hypocrisy), where there is integrity of heart you not only see God but you begin to see the world as God sees it. The scribes and the Pharisees looked out on the publicans and sinners and saw rebels. You know what Jesus saw? Lost sheep; lost people who needed new life. If you want to get a God-like vision of our world, be pure in heart. Then you shall see God, and through His eyes shall see the world. It will transform your sight.

A few members of our congregation have experienced eye surgery. It's a marvelous surgery. Through this provision of medical science people have been enabled to see, and see well. It's a miracle of science. It is a provision of the grace of God that those of us who have our eyes clouded, who are tapping our way through life, can now—through an openness to the cleansing, purifying power of God, through His Spirit, through the blood of the cross, and through the power of His Word—walk with new sight, and see Him. "Blessed are the pure in heart, for they shall see God."

For Further Study

1. What does it mean to be "pure in heart"?

2. Toward whom are our hearts to be "pure"? Why?

3. This sixth Beatitude promises a vision of God. When and how can we see God? Why is this promise of a vision important to your spiritual walk?

Note

D. Martyn Lloyd-Jones, *Studies in the Sermon on the Mount* (Grand Rapids: Wm. B. Eerdmans Publishing Co., 1977), p. 114.

CHAPTER EIGHT

The Peace Child

Matthew 5:9

If someone were to come to earth from another planet with the assignment to discover what Earth's primary business is, what do you think his report would say? I think it probably would be, "The chief industry of earth is war. That's what they engage themselves in more than anything else."

Professor Quincy Wright, in his book, *A Study of War*, lists by country the number of wars there were between the years 1480-1941: Great Britain, 78; France, 71; Spain, 64; Russia, 61; Austria, 52; Germany, 23; China, 11; Japan, 9; the United States, 13. But lest we become overly confident, we had 110 wars—often ruthless ones—with the American Indians during that period.[1]

"Blessed are the peacemakers, for they shall be

called sons of God" (Matt. 5:9). The Bible is a book about peace, with some 400 separate references to the word *peace*. It speaks of peace between people, peace between nations, peace of God. Yet peace is a scarce, unusual, elusive commodity. There's very little of it. If you don't believe me, just spend an hour watching the news. One thing after another—murder, slayings, trouble, crises—very little good news.

Peace—An Elusive Commodity

Many of you reading this book are at war within yourself. You may be in conflict with your employer; you hate the thought of Monday morning. Some of you are in conflict with teachers, or students, or school administrators. Some of you are in conflict with your husband or wife, maybe with your children. Wars without; wars within—we are a people of conflict.

What is the source of conflict? What causes it? One big word with only three letters—SIN. The problem is at the heart of man. Basic to our nature are selfishness, pride and greed—we aren't simply a needy people, sometimes we are a greedy people. Our human hearts are desperately wicked and they drive us to want and possess selfish interests. This desire gets us into conflict when we come across people who already have what we want and we enter into war and battle for those things.

Listen to what James says about the subject: "What is the source of quarrels and conflicts among you? Is not the source your pleasures that wage war in your members? You lust and do not have; so you commit murder. And you are envious and cannot obtain; so you fight and quarrel. You do not have because you do not ask. You ask and do not receive, because you ask with wrong motives, so that you may spend it on your pleasures" (Jas. 4:1-3).

Sin expresses itself in three wars, according to James. (1) we're at war with one another; (2) we're at war within; (3) we're at war with God. But the war actually begins when we are at war with God, or as James says, in "hostility toward God" (v. 4). War with God creates war within our own selves—manifested by lust and envy; this breaks out in war between each other. Sin has left its indelible mark upon us; we're selfish, pursuing selfish, personal interests.

Then the devil comes around in the form of troublemakers and stirs us up. Some people are either in conflict themselves or they create it. Do you know people like that? You see them coming and you say, "Oh, oh—here comes trouble!" These people are the devil's little ambassadors, and they're called troublemakers, not peacemakers, because they create conflict.

Peacemakers—An Exclusive Company

Peacemakers are an exclusive group; there aren't many of them around. Jesus said, "Blessed are the peacemakers." Martyn Lloyd-Jones says, "Why are peacemakers blessed? The answer is that they are blessed because they are so absolutely unlike everybody else."[2] You don't find many of those folks around. Just a few. It's much easier to be a troublemaker, one who stirs things up; throws a little fuel on a fire; adds to gossip. That's a troublemaker—creating unrest, adding to conflict.

A peacemaker is one who strives to prevent contention, strife and discord, who uses his or her influence to reconcile enemies. Now your *enemy* could be your husband or wife, parent, child—anyone with whom you are in strife. A peacemaker is one who brings together, holds back contention, reconciles. Dag Hammarskjold was committed to bringing peace among nations. In his writings you see a man who by nature wanted peace in our world, and he gave himself to bringing it about.

Do you remember the closing scene in the movie "Ben Hur"? Judah Ben Hur was a man of strife, conflict, and discord; then he met Jesus. His comment was, "Jesus took the sword out of my hand." When Jesus comes along He takes a hurting person and makes him a healer. He takes the sword out of our hands, and makes us instruments of His peace. A peacemaker is one who has put down the sword and goes into the midst of conflict to reconcile and bring together.

Being a peacemaker is very demanding. Some people who sound the call of "peace, peace" when there is no peace are false prophets of peace. Real peace costs something; it takes and demands: (1) humility, (2) activism, (3) risk.

Being a peacemaker requires, that a person first be humble. He must take the one who is number one on his agenda, "me," and place himself near the bottom of the list. At the top, in the number one spot, he puts others. A peacemaker is one who is willing to put his priorities aside and be involved in the concerns and relationships of others. That takes humility. Peacemakers cannot be cocky, confident, proud people who move around in their own world saying, "I want my way at any cost." No, they say, "I want the best for them, and I'm willing to pay the price." A peacemaker puts others first.

Another demand of a peacemaker is that he or she be an activist. That word has come to mean "political troublemaker" in our culture; but it's a good word with a good meaning. A peacemaker has to be actively practicing making peace among others.

There are several words in the Scriptures in both Hebrew and Greek which we translate *peace* in our English versions of the Bible. One of these, *shalom* in the Hebrew, is widely used as a greeting in our Jewish communities today. *Shalom* is found in the books of Ezra (4:17; 5:7) and Daniel (4:1; 6:25) in the form of a blessing, "May your peace [shalom] abound."

In the New Testament we find the Greek *eirene*—which means peace, quietness, rest, set at one again. This is the kind of peace Jesus promised in John 14:27: "Peace I leave with you; My peace I give to you; not as the world gives, do I give to you." It's the peace Paul speaks of as the fruit of the Spirit: "love, joy, peace [eirene], . . . against such things there is no law" (Gal. 5:22,23).

A kindred word to *shalom* is *salem*. You've seen churches called Salem Lutheran or Salem Baptist. That words means peace. The word means not simply the absence of conflict; it means the presence of that which is good and positive and building. So when a person says "shalom" to you, he's not saying, "I hope you don't have any problems," he's saying, "I hope you have prosperity and a good life."

The concept of a peacemaker is of one who is actively involved, who goes into the midst of conflict. He is not just a peace lover, he is a peacemaker—one who goes into a situation and tackles the problem, who deals with the things that create conflict. If you're content to simply watch and applaud peace, you're a peace lover but not necessarily a peacemaker. To be a peacemaker takes positive, active involvement, initiative; it takes thrusting yourself into the lives of others.

Being a peacemaker also involves risk. A peacemaker is easily misunderstood. He may enter conflict between people and they'll say, "None of your business, get out of here!" But that's the cost of being a peacemaker. You may be misunderstood, or be accused of getting in the way.

A peacemaker is also someone who does not offer easy forgiveness. Luke 17:3 says: "If your brother sins, rebuke him; and if he repents, forgive him." That is to say you don't go into a situation and forgive people who are at odds unless they've repented. That doesn't sound as if the peacemaker is very forgiving, but a peacemaker is supposed to rebuke sin; then he forgives when the sinner repents. Now that is risky. It's much easier to say, "I forgive you." That's cheap. That doesn't cost anything. That isn't caring; that's just throwing something over it to cover it up; a Band-Aid over a major infection. It's the same thing when you say, "I'm sorry" and don't really mean it. You say a cheap, "I'm sorry" and you don't deal with the issue.

You'll be misunderstood if you come into a situation of conflict and take the steps necessary to make peace. You don't forgive unless there's repentance; and you're not going to be appreciated for it. Yet that's the price of real peace. But there's a great delight in peacemaking. It's the privilege of bringing health where there's hurt, of bringing together those who are alienated. What a great opportunity it is to be a peacemaker.

Peacemaking—An Extensive Field

There are four general areas where the peacemaker becomes involved in conflict: (1) the community, (2) at work, (3) at church, (4) at home.

A peacemaker's field includes the community where he lives. In our city of Whittier, California, there has been a minor furor over the young people "cruising" along

Whittier Boulevard. We have watched with interest as people have taken sides on the issue. There are those who have done nothing but express anger and concern over the whole situation—objecting to the noise, disturbance of peace, increase of crime, etc. They've offered nothing but objection.

Then there are those who have risen up and sought to bring peace between the young people and the merchants, residents and police department. I applaud their attempts. They have asked, "What has created this situation? Maybe we haven't provided enough for our young people to do. Maybe we need more programs and greater athletic opportunities so that the young people don't have empty time to fill with 'cruising down the boulevard.' "

A committee formed to take some action. Of course, they've been misunderstood and maligned from both sides—that's the price of peacemaking. Even though he is misunderstood, a peacemaker attempts to resolve conflicts in his community. I challenge you to community involvement as a peacemaker, doing the work of God.

A peacemaker may have to do his peacemaking at work, on the job. When there is a conflict between employer and employee, or between labor and management, the peacemaker has to stand in the breach and be able to link hands and bring people together; to bring understanding. He may be misunderstood, it may be risky, but peacemakers are the chosen few who rise up as sons of God. It's worth it. It's a God-like task.

Peacemakers even have to serve as peacemakers in their church. I served a church where there were two men at odds with each other, and had been as long as I could remember. If one man was in favor of something, the other opposed it, and vice versa. Often church problems are not theological—although we put theological labels on them—they're personality conflicts. We just call them theological problems to make them sound legitimate. But I watched these two men limp through life because they were not at peace with each other. It was tough to bring them together; and I don't know that they still are.

Any time there is a conflict between God's people in a church, how tragic it is. It denies both of them the privilege of total worship and delight in their Lord and of fellowship with each other. When we can effect peace between God's people, what a beautiful thing that is.

Peacemakers are needed in the home. I don't know what goes on in your home, but I'm sure you occasionally need someone who must act as a peacemaker between your family members.

There is one group in America today that has made more of home life than anyone else has. I find their theology way out in left field and the history of their beginnings very strange. There is nothing in their belief that I can relate to Christianity as the Bible teaches it, yet the Mormons have an enormous appeal to many. It's my conviction that the reason for this is that they have brought the family together as a unit: peaceful, united and loving—to all outward appearances. And I've got to applaud them for that. When they outdistance us, it's to our shame. There ought to be peace in our homes and we ought to work at it.

Donald G. Barnhouse talks about marriage being like two separate planets—each going in its own orbit, at its own speed—that all of a sudden are brought into the same orbit, at the same speed.[3] That's an incredible task. But that's what marriage requires—two people getting into the same orbit, at the same speed. If they continue to move off in their own independent areas, there is going to be an interplanetary collision. When you have a breakdown of peace in the home, the breakdown of the community and of the nation follows. Peace begins at home.

Peacemakers—The Exceptional Children

The peacemakers are blessed because "they shall be called sons of God" (Matt. 5:9). The peacemaker is a son of God because God is *the* Peacemaker. God is the source of peace. Six times in the New Testament He is called the God of peace. That's His title. First Corinthians 14:33 reminds us that "God is not a God of confusion but of peace"; He is the very author of it. He is the foundation for peace. As we read in Galatians 5:22, the fruit of the Spirit is peace. It's a God-like gift. He is a

God of peace. Paul writes in Ephesians 2:15 that God establishes peace and in Colossians 1:20 that He "made peace through the blood of" Jesus Christ. He is the source of peace, He is the one who creates peace, He is the giver of peace, He is the author of peace.

So the blessing of being a peacemaker is simply that we are noted for our God-likeness. We are sons of God; therefore, we are God-like when we are peacemakers. We resemble God. We act as God acts when we are peacemakers. We do what God does. The blessing of the peacemaker is that he resembles his Father. A child who does not resemble his father—in action and in nature—is a shame to the father.

While leading some meetings at Wheaton College I met one young man who was a delight. He told me his name was Steve—he was a sophomore. I'll tell you one thing, his motor was running. I like to see someone who's charged up and ready to go. All you need to do is direct him. Steve was one of these folks who has the world in front of him and he was anxious to get out and win people for Christ. He had missed a session I led and he said "I just want you to tell me what you said to the folks there." Well, I don't see many college sophomores that excited so I told him what I said.

He told me, "You know, I have a decision to make: whether to go out and witness in churches in evangelism, or to accept an offer as a youth pastor in a church." We talked about his future. He said, "I have a heart to go out across America and bring people to Christ."

I asked, "What does your dad do?"

He replied, "My dad's a pastor in the southeastern part of the country." It turned out that his father and I were in a gospel team together in college and he became one of the finest evangelists in America. He used church-centered evangelism, going out and winning thousands of people to Christ. He had strong ministry and is now serving a large Presbyterian Church.

Here was a boy who looked just like his dad. "Blessed are the peacemakers, for they shall be called sons of God." When you are a peacemaker, you look like your Father. Blessed are those who make peace; they resemble their heavenly Father.

The Challenge to Your Life

Do you know some conflict that needs resolving? Are you presently at odds with another? A mate? A child? A parent? Your employer? An employee? A classmate? Are you willing to do the God-like thing and go and risk making peace?

"Blessed are the peacemakers."

For Further Study

1. What are the major sources of conflict between individuals? Nations? Man and God?

2. What are the actual requirements and functions of a peacemaker as discussed in this Beatitude? Why are these individuals called "blessed"?

3. What are some risks peacemakers must face?

4. Do you think every believer is called to be a peacemaker? Why or why not?

Notes
1. Billy Graham, *The Secret of Happiness!* (New York: Pocket Books, 1955), p. 141.
2. D. Martyn Lloyd-Jones, *Studies in the Sermon on the Mount* (Grand Rapids: Wm. B. Eerdmans Publishing Co., 1977), p. 119.
3. James Montgomery Boice, *The Sermon on the Mount* (Grand Rapids: Zondervan Publishing Co., 1972), p. 54.

CHAPTER NINE

He Never Promised Us a Rose Garden

Matthew 5:10-12

Jesus didn't come to make life easy: He came to make men great. The eighth Beatitude says: "Blessed are those who have been persecuted for the sake of righteousness, for theirs is the kingdom of heaven. Blessed are you when men revile you, and persecute you, and say all kinds of evil against you falsely, on account of Me. Rejoice, and be glad, for your reward in heaven is great, for so they persecuted the prophets who were before you" (Matt. 5:10-12).

When you look at this Beatitude you are again confronted with one of those outstanding qualities of the ministry of Jesus: Jesus was always up front, candid, honest. He never said, "Follow Me; it will be easy." If there was going to be trouble, He said so. If His followers were going to be persecuted, He said so. No surprises with Jesus.

That isn't always the case with His followers, however. When we want someone to follow us, or take a job, or buy a product, we present it in its best light. We make the case a little more attractive than it really is. When our church needed a junior high youth sponsor we would have gotten one easily if we had advertised, "They're all very responsive; there are no discipline problems; they all are anxious to serve God; you'll never have any difficulty on socials; they're always on time." Sounds good; not true! Jesus never did that. He would rather thin out the crowds at the beginning. He told them, "It's tough; you'll be persecuted; you're going to face pressures and problems—that's the way it is."

Persecution—A Reality of History

Persecution of the church of Jesus Christ is a historical reality. The verb "to persecute" means to put to flight, to drive away, to pursue. It's the same word that describes how you pursue a flying enemy. Have you ever sat down to eat, or enjoy a good book, when a fly started to buzz around your ear?

I was in New York one time and there must have been thousands of flies. They came through the chimney, through holes in the screens, through the door every time it was opened—I felt like I was in a war. Every time I went after one I was *persecuting* him— that's the verb: To go after; to get after a flying enemy; to pursue; to persecute that fly as best you know how! If that fly could talk it would say, "I've been persecuted;

you've gone after me with a swatter; you've attempted to take my life; you really have vexed me." The word persecute means to pursue to give you trouble; to oppress you; to vex you because of your faith.

Now, at this point we had better distinguish the difference between punishment and persecution—they are not the same. Punishment is what good people do to you for doing evil. Persecution is what evil men do to you for doing good. You're not persecuted when you pay a ticket for speeding. That's punishment. But when you stand up for God and you're oppressed, that's persecution.

The Christian church has a long history of being persecuted. To the best of our knowledge all of the apostles, except two, were martyred. Judas, of course, killed himself and the apostle John died of old age. The apostles were crucified upside down, speared, beheaded—that's persecution.

The apostle Paul tells about his persecutions: "In far more labors, in far more imprisonments, beaten times without number, often in danger of death. Five times I received from the Jews thirty-nine lashes. Three times I was beaten with rods, once I was stoned, three times I was shipwrecked, a night and a day I have spent in the deep. I have been on frequent journeys, in dangers from rivers, dangers from robbers, dangers from my countrymen, dangers from the Gentiles, dangers in the city, dangers in the wilderness, dangers on the sea, dangers among false brethren; I have been in labor and hardship, through many sleepless nights, in hunger and thirst, often without food, in cold and exposure. Apart from such external things, there is the daily pressure upon me of concern for all the churches" (2 Cor. 11:23-28).

In the year 1415 John Hus, a church reformer, was burned at the stake for his faith, and from John Hus until present-day missionaries serving the Lord among "uncivilized" peoples a trail of blood marks the persecution of the Christian church. In the early years of church history, during the Roman persecution, Nero, one of the vilest of them all in terms of his ideas, covered the believers with pitch then set them afire; human torches to light his garden. He wrapped Christians in the skins of wild animals and threw them to his hunting dogs to be torn, mangled and eaten.

The Beatitude says that they will "say all kinds of evil against you falsely, on account of Me." That was certainly true in the early church. Members of the early church were persecuted as a result of (1) slander—they were accused of immorality, and (2) the political situation—they opposed the emperor.

There were four slanderous accusations brought against the early church: They were accused of being (1) cannibalistic; (2) immoral; (3) incendiary; (4) home wreckers.

The Christians were accused of being cannibals because Jesus told them at the Last Supper, "Drink . . . My blood of the covenant, which is to be shed on behalf of many" (Matt. 26:27,28). Their accusers knew the Christians did not literally drink blood, but they used whatever they could to stop Christianity.

The Christians were accused of being immoral because they gathered together to have *agape* (love) feasts. They kissed one another ("Greet one another with a holy kiss," Rom. 16:16; 1 Cor. 16:20; 2 Cor. 13:12; 1 Pet. 5:14); the perverted minds of their enemies took this to mean that they had licentious gatherings.

The Christians were said to be incendiary because they were always talking about the earth being destroyed by fire. Their enemies said that they were planning an insurrection; that they were trying to destroy everything that was stable and established; that they said everything would go up in flames. The believers, of course, were speaking of the new heaven and new earth, and that the old heaven and earth would be destroyed by fire.

The believers were accused of breaking up homes and destroying families with their belief. You know how it goes: if one member of the family becomes a believer and the other members do not, then a rift is created between the family members. Sometimes believing in Christ truly did break up families, but most often the non-believers cast out the believer.

Christians were also persecuted for political reasons. The emperor finally came to the place where he claimed to be a god. Once a year the people under the rule of the emperor were required to burn a small amount of incense and confess publicly that "Caesar is Lord." The Christians could not do that—there was only one Lord, Jesus Christ, and they would not bow down nor confess that the emperor was Lord. This of course led to their being persecuted.

One book I read commented that Christians today don't really experience persecution. I don't think that's true. Across the world there are Christians right now who are in concentration camps because of their faith. Right now there are Christians who are facing persecution, loss of jobs, loss of income because of their faith. Some have been beaten as a result of their Christian testimony; they have been alienated from their families. There are Christians right now in parts of our world, often in Communist or Moslem countries, who are being persecuted because of their faith in much the same way the early church was.

Let me suggest other ways Christians are persecuted. If you stand up for God and for righteousness, you will soon discover that some will sneer in a way that says, "You prude." There is a kind of social buffeting that says, "All right, be standoffish, don't laugh at our jokes." I know a businessman who took a job as an executive in a company and he is really going through it because he refuses to drink. Executives above him continue to pressure him to "join the rest of us" and drink. He is having a difficult time, but he says, "I never felt so strongly about it before as I do now that I have to stand up for it."

Persecution takes the form of ridicule for the kid on the campus who refuses to pop the pills. It takes the form of ostracism; you're set apart—"What are you, do you think you're better than we are?" Loss of friends, mockery.

Persecution—A Companion of Godliness

Now, there are some valid reasons why Christians are persecuted. Sometimes it's because we're weird! We're just strange. We're supposed to be a peculiar people, but that means distinctive, not weird.

When I see Christians do dumb things and then appeal on the grounds that they've been persecuted for righteousness' sake I remind them that there is no promise in the Word of God that because we're bizarre we're blessed. If you try to force a tract on someone and they don't want it and they mock you for it, then you aren't being persecuted for righteousness' sake, you're being persecuted for foolishness' sake! We're not in the world to bludgeon people into the kingdom.

When in your own folly you bring ridicule on yourself and on the church, that's not the same as being persecuted for righteousness' sake. When you act foolish, or bizarre, or objectionable, or you're a nuisance, that's not proper grounds for being delighted that you're being persecuted for righteousness.

I think the classic story comes to us right out of Joe

Bayly's book, *The Gospel Blimp*. Some people in the community decide that they are going to let their town know about the gospel. So they develop a blimp—not the Goodyear; this is the Gospel Blimp. It floats over the town dropping gospel bombs—tracts. The town patiently puts up with it. However, soon the Christians decide that some of the town is not paying attention, so they put a sound system in the blimp. This time the newspaper has something to say about "the airborne sound truck—the invader of our privacy." Then the folks who develop the Gospel Blimp go around blaring their message at football games and all other town events. When the townspeople sabotage the sound system, the blimp builders cry that they are being persecuted for righteousness' sake. That's not being persecuted for righteousness' sake—that's being persecuted for being bizarre!

You don't win the world by invading their privacy. You don't win the world by being foolish in that sense. There are valid reasons why we've sometimes been persecuted. Colleen Townsend Evans, in her book *A New Joy*, says, "Most of my suffering has come from doing something wrong. . . . There is no joy in this kind of pain."[1]

However, "All who desire to live godly in Christ Jesus will be persecuted" (2 Tim. 3:18). Universal acceptance and popularity are companions to false prophets and carnality. Any time you are totally accepted, you're in trouble. Jesus told His disciples,

"Woe to you when all men speak well of you" (Luke 6:26). Maybe you work hard at it, and finally they all speak well of you. Now that's trouble. If nobody is ever offended by your standards; if nobody ever ridicules you because of your convictions and your life-style and how you stand up for morality and honesty and integrity; if you're never made fun of, never ridiculed—then you're in trouble. "Woe to you when all men speak well of you."

John Stott says, "Persecution is simply the clash of two irreconcilable value systems." That of the believer and that of the unbeliever. You just can't put those two together. You see, the true church of Jesus Christ becomes the conscience for all the people. And how do you deal with an uneasy conscience? You try to put it down, to silence it.

The Christian has an irreconcilable value system in contrast to the world system—which is to get by, to succeed at any cost. When the Christian system comes against the world system it will always bring us into conflict: those who are under the gun of God's righteousness will try to put us down, because righteousness creates uneasiness in their lives. The true church of Jesus Christ will have to say yes at times while others are saying no. We may say no when others say yes, and we clash. You see, we're strangers and pilgrims and aliens, and most people don't put out a welcome mat for aliens. There's something different about us, and the human response is to handle differences by objecting to them.

Bonhoeffer, you may recall, was a German theologian who opposed Hitler. As a Christian and as a leading theologian in Germany he felt he had to stand up against Hitler and the whole Nazi philosophy—he just could not stomach it. And he did stand against it and publicly speak against it. He was then imprisoned. In prison he lost his status as a teacher. He also underwent persecution in the camp and his family was punished. But he said, "I cannot change my convictions. I must make them known. I must stand." He died three or four days before the liberation in 1945. He gave his life. He made a statement to the effect that all who live godly lives must suffer persecution. His own life was a testimony to that statement.

When there are conflicting value systems, you may never be confined to a concentration camp but you will have conflict. And if you experience no conflict, no tension, no pressure, that ought to drive you to your knees, just as persecution would.

It's interesting that the word *righteous* comes from a word which means "to cut, to divide." Righteousness has a way of doing that; it divides people. It cuts us apart; it sets us apart. It is inevitable in the Christian life. It's not very popular in our kind of world. Persecution is a reality that accompanies godliness.

Persecution—A Source of Joy

"Rejoice, and be glad." We're not to retaliate in the face of persecution. We're not to sulk. We're not to lick our wounds in self-pity like a dog. We're not even to grin and bear it like a stoic. The text simply says we are to "Rejoice," leap for joy. You may be thinking, "You're out of your head! When was the last time you celebrated persecution? People don't have parties to celebrate persecution." Yet the Lord Jesus has the audacity to say, "Rejoice, and be glad." Cheer as we're being persecuted. How come? Why should we rejoice at persecution? There are four reasons.

We should rejoice when we are persecuted because persecution is a certificate of authenticity. It's the real thing. Notice what verse 3 says: "Blessed are the poor in spirit, for theirs is the kingdom of heaven." I mentioned that it is those who humble themselves, who realize they are spiritually bankrupt, who are candidates for His kingdom. That's the first Beatitude—theirs is the kingdom of heaven. The last Beatitude says, "Blessed are those who have been persecuted for the sake of righteousness, for theirs is the kingdom of heaven."

All of the Beatitudes are for those who are a part of His kingdom and His reign, and the persecuted are those who are His own family. It's a mark of authenticity. If you don't have it, you better question your sonship. It's a label. You're part of the family. Look what you're experiencing.

A second reason we ought to rejoice is that it is a perfecting of the believer. Peter, in his first Epistle, tells us that all the temptations and trials and persecutions the believer goes through are all a way of refining us, like gold put through the fire. It is a refining; it is a perfecting of the child of God.

Billy Graham tells of a friend who lost everything in the depression of the thirties—his job, a huge estate, his wife, he even lost his home. But he had a tenacious faith. It was tough, but he held in there with his Lord. Everything was gone. He said that one day the man was walking along in New York City and saw that they were building a huge church of stone. He watched for a while. Then he noticed a workman who was chipping away at a triangular piece of stone. The Christian had time on his hands, so he went up and asked the man, "What are you doing?"

The workman pointed to a triangular-shaped space up by the steeple and commented: "I'm shaping this down here so that it will fit up there." And Graham said his friend felt that it was just as if God had spoken through the mason. "I'm shaping it down here so that it will fit up there."

Maybe you've known a little bit of that shaping. I don't believe that God sends problems into our lives; but He permits them so that we can be shaped, developed and perfected. A Christian without pressure, without persecution, is a soft Christian. There's a strength and virility and dynamic that comes only under heat and pressure. The perfecting of the believer—shaping him down here that he might fit up there.

The third reason for us to rejoice is because of the nearness of Christ. One of the things we discover is that when the test gets really severe, He is also near. It follows. Remember the three men in the fire—Shadrach, Meshach and Abednego? There they were; yet they were protected. There was also a fourth person in the fire with them—like the Son of God. We believe it was a pre-incarnate presence of Jesus Christ Himself.

The Lord is with us in those fires and those tests. You may go through life with its ease and its delight and never be aware of His presence. But when you go through the pits and you bottom out and go through some testing and trial, you discover what you never discovered before: that the Lord is right there with His people. What a delight to know that "even though I walk through the valley of the shadow of death, I fear no evil; for Thou art with me" (Ps. 23:4).

The last reason to rejoice and be glad is the promise of reward. Notice what Matthew 5:12 says: "Rejoice, and be glad, for your reward in heaven is great." You may lose it here, but you'll gain it there. You may be tested here, but you'll be rewarded there.

Now, I know it once was fashionable for Christians to say we don't want rewards, but Abraham sought the reward of the city whose maker and builder was God; Moses gave up his Egyptian heritage and suffered as an Israelite because he looked for the reward; Jesus, according to Hebrews 12:2, because of the joy that was set before Him, the reward of joy, endured the cross.

It's never wrong to, in the name of righteousness, seek the reward. It's written all the way through the Word of God. We shall stand before Him and receive the blessing of His "well done." The reward is great. You may go through persecution here, but if you're faithful to God, there is the promise of reward.

The Challenge to Your Life

Where are you today? Are you maybe being persecuted for the wrong reasons? We are to be harmless as doves but wise as serpents (see Matt. 10:16). Or maybe you're not persecuted at all, and that ought to trouble you. Why aren't you persecuted? Have you so blended into the environment that you're not distinctive?

A model for us is Daniel in the Old Testament. He was young when he went to Babylon. There were certain areas in himself where he would have to change; there were things he would have to do; but there were certain things he would not do. He allowed the Babylonians to change his name, as did his three friends. He also allowed himself—with his friends—to learn Chaldean arts and sciences. But when it came to a life-style change, Daniel said, "I draw the line." Very quietly, but unashamedly, Daniel stood up for righteousness' sake. What did they say about him? "He's a troubler. He makes us look bad. We've got to do him in."

That's always the case when you stand for God. You look different.

> Dare to be a Daniel!
> Dare to stand alone!
> Dare to have a purpose firm!
> Dare to make it known.[2]

Those who so stand shall be persecuted, not because they're foolish, not because they're unwise, but because they're righteous.

"Blessed are those who have been persecuted for the sake of "righteousness."

For Further Study

1. Explain what you see the difference to be between punishment and persecution.

2. Is it possible to be a growing Christian and not be experiencing persecution? Explain.

3. What are some reasons why you think Christians are persecuted?

4. How is it possible to celebrate in persecution?

Note

1. Colleen Townsend Evans, *A New Joy* (Old Tappan, NJ: Fleming H. Revell Co., 1973), p. 107.
2. "Dare to Be a Daniel" by Philip Bliss, *Everyone Sings*, (Ventura, CA: Praise Book Publications, 1966), p. 95.

CHAPTER TEN

Why God Put Us Here

Matthew 5:13-16

We now move from the Beatitudes, the first part of the Sermon on the Mount in which our Lord spells out the character of the church, to the next section which speaks of our influence in the world today.

Have you ever asked yourself, "Why am I here? What am I doing here? Why did God put me here?" Does life sometimes seem rather meaningless and you feel as if you're in a maze and can't make any sense or rhyme or reason out of the whole affair? You sense kind of an indecision, an indefiniteness, and you really want to know, "What in the world is my function in the world—if, in fact, I have one?"

Jesus answered that question in Matthew 5, verses 13-16, through two metaphors: "You are the salt of the earth. . . . You are the light of the world." The believer is placed in the world for the world's sake.

Normative Christianity

I can see Jesus as He was in His own home. Again and again He watched His mother put salt into the meat to keep it from spoiling and He saw her taking care of the little light that kept their home illuminated. These two activities in the home in Jesus' day were very basic, and Jesus says that's what we as Christians are—basic, normative. Life just doesn't function without us. We are the light; we are the salt.

Jesus says we are distinctive. When Jesus said that we are the salt of the earth, He didn't mean to imply that we are part of the earth, that we are one and the same. Although we are salt, we are not a part of the world; we are not to be confused. "You are the light of the world," but the light and the world are separate. Light is for the world but they are not one and the same. Salt is for the earth, but salt is not the earth. You and the world are distinguishable—you are not to be confused. You are distinct, you are separate from it. Stott says, "You're as different as chalk and cheese." Now if you wake up in the middle of the night when you're hungry and take a chunk of chalk, thinking you have cheese, you would know what he means. Chalk has no taste; cheese does.

Richard Quebedeaux has written a provocative volume, *The Worldly Evangelicals* which states that we live in the kind of a world where you can't really tell who's Christian and who's not. It's kind of fashionable for the Christian to have just enough of the world so that he can move around without being distinctive. But Jesus says, "You're not of it, you are salt for it, you are light in it. Keep separate. Keep distinct."

With that distinction comes a responsibility. In Greek there is the emphatic pronoun "you" that says, "You and you only are the salt of the earth; you and you only are the light of the world." The implication is that if you are not being salt where you are, then that part of the world is not salted; if you are not being a light in your part of the world, then there is no illumination there. You, and only you, have a distinct responsibility. You are a living influence. You don't simply *bring* salt and light, you don't simply *have* salt to share and light to disseminate darkness, you *are* salt, you *are* light. It is not something you have, it's something you are.

If you ever take a trip to the Holy Land, you will discover a place called Qumran. This area to the north and west of the Dead Sea is very arid. It was here that a little shepherd boy threw a stone up into a cave and heard the sound of pottery smashing, which led to the discovery of the Dead Sea Scrolls; the Word of God, hundreds of years old, coming right out of the first century. The community that lived there was called the Essenes, the "sons of light." Talk about a tragedy, you know what these "sons of light" did? They had the Word of God but they got off to themselves and holed up; they deprived the rest of the world of the light and used it only for themselves, so that the rest of the world was left in darkness. The Essenes chose to separate themselves from the darkness of the world and light up only themselves.

We are to be distinct but not isolated; we are to be involved with the world, salting it and shedding light in it.

Have you ever noticed that all the metaphors of the New Testament speak of the church as being penetrating? the military metaphor—penetrate the enemy; light penetrates darkness; salt penetrates meat and flavors it and preserves it. We don't *bring* salt and light; we *are* salt and light.

Subtle Christian Influence

There are two ways in which Christians influence the world: (1) in a subtle way, as salt and (2) in an obvious way, as light. The subtle Christian influence is the salt of the earth.

How big is your salt shaker at home. Just a little object in comparison to other items in your home. It may be a very fancy salt shaker, but it's not very big. The reason for this is that it doesn't take very much at a time to do the job. But did you ever try to eat a meal without it? Some of you who are on a salt-free diet have, but you sure used salt substitutes if you could. Salt is small, but it makes its presence known.

How is salt used? How does it influence you? Let me name three ways: (1) salt produces thirst; (2) salt provides flavor; (3) salt preserves food.

Did you ever eat a good ham dinner? It seems you

can't get enough to drink when you eat ham. The salt in the ham creates thirst. When was the last time you made the world thirst for Jesus? Or maybe you never have. Do people see you and your life and say, "He has something I'd like. He whets my appetite for God!"? Salt makes people thirsty. A Christian influence makes people thirsty for God.

Salt provides flavor. Without Christianity and the impact of God and the flavor He brings to life, the world is insipid, tasteless, bland. It needs the zest and tang that the Christian brings to it. The excitement the world brings is not satisfying; if you don't believe it, just ask someone who's "done it all." The thrills of the world don't last; there is always a search for something more; something new; further excitement. What the world provides is like eating Chinese food. We kid about Chinese food—that we can eat a big Chinese dinner and two hours later feel like we could eat another meal. It seems that Chinese food just doesn't stay with us too long. It's very good but it doesn't last. That's the way the pleasures of the world are.

The world accuses Christianity of not being exciting, of being bland. Why does the world say things like that? Where is the salt?

Sometimes the world accuses the church of being depressing. Robert Louis Stevenson once entered in his diary, "I have been to church today, and am not depressed"; as if such a result was very extraordinary. Where is the saltiness?

Do people see you and say, "Well, here comes another 'Christian'—depression time!" What we need is the kind of Christianity that comes into the world and makes it say, "Hey, that's zesty, tangy. That's something that really flavors this insipid world."

Salt also preserves; it prevents decay. For centuries salt was the principal preservative of meat. Rubbing it into meat stops decay and rottenness. It cannot change corrupt food into fresh food, or rotten food into good food, but it puts the brakes on the process of decaying. In the same way salt is rubbed into meat to stop decay, the Christian needs to penetrate the world to stop the process of decay. And as long as the salt is in the box or in the shaker it will have no effect on food; and as long as the Christian stays in his smug little corner he will have no influence on the world. There doesn't have to be much salting in the church, because we are already salt; but we need to be out in the world, in society, rubbing into the life around us to preserve it.

I've seen more than one Christian in a business who stood up for God and brought a screeching halt to questionable practices of advertising, questionable techniques of salesmanship and a whole process of activities that had gone along unchecked. The Christian doesn't have to blare a trumpet, or beat a drum, or clang a cymbal—he can quietly, firmly, incessantly, subtly do his job of being salt. When the world gets rotten, when the meat begins to spoil, nobody blames the meat. The question is, "Where was the salt?"

Unless you're a first-time visitor from another planet or you've been in hibernation since 1913, you don't have to be told that the world is in desperate need of salt. Read your paper. It has enough rottenness to use up all the salt there is on earth. Jesus looked out on His world and cared, and because He cared He said, "Something needs to be done to bring a halt to all this." Salt was needed because sin had left its mark on the world.

Now you can abuse salt. Jesus goes on to say, "You are the salt of the earth; but if the salt has become tasteless, how will it be made salty again?" There are several opinions about what Jesus meant here, because, strictly speaking, sodium chloride is about as stable a chemical compound as you'll find. You can allow pure sodium chloride to stand and stand, and it will resist all infiltration of anything, because it is a very stable chemical compound. Then how can it lose its saltiness? Well, one way is to mix it with other spices so that it loses some of its power; the salt is still there, but other tastes are there also.

Another explanation is that in the eastern countries often the salt was not pure, it was mixed with other minerals from the mine and that would decrease its saltiness. But whatever the explanation is, when salt loses its flavor, it is good for nothing but to be thrown out in the pathway where people walk, not on good soil where nothing could grow because of its presence.

Whenever the Christian allows worldly values to infiltrate his life, whenever he lets other things interfere with his Christian life, whenever he becomes part of the world, suddenly he's tasteless. He becomes diluted, powerless, of no use.

Obvious Christian Influence

There's a more obvious form of Christian influence: "You are the light of the world." You may have a little salt shaker around the house and hardly notice it; but when you've got a light, that's obvious. I can imagine Jesus looking out on His world and seeing cities built on hills, as they are in Judea. You can't hide those little cities. There they are, built on the sides of mountains and on the sides of hills all over Judea. You see them from a distance. Light is like that. It's difficult to hide light. If you light a match in a very dark room, you see it. Light is obvious.

The world is wrapped in darkness, in gloom. It has chosen darkness. There is spiritual darkness because it has turned its back on Jesus Christ, who is light. There is educational darkness, because the educational system has asked God to stay home. There is social darkness, because folks don't like Him at the table. We have darkness in our world because we have chosen to leave out the Light of Life. God says of His Son, "I have sent Him into the world as light." Jesus said, "I am the light of the world."

Following through with this metaphor of light as it relates to the Christian life, light has two qualities: it illumines and it reflects.

Light illumines; it shares its light. Light dispels darkness and shows us truth. When the light comes on, all of a sudden everything becomes obvious. Whenever the light comes on it reveals things that need to be cared for. That's the nature of light. Light, historically and biblically, is *enlightenment* and enlightenment always relates to the truth. Isn't it interesting that some of the periods of history were called ages of enlightenment, particularly the eighteenth century? That means that understanding was enlarged. People began to see the truth.

When Jesus says that we are the light of the world, He is saying that the Christian comes to reveal the truth. We are in the world to share the light that Jesus Christ can free those who are in bondage. It is possible for the world to be won to Him, to live the liberated life in the freedom of the grace of God.

Not only is it the nature of light to illumine, but also to reflect. Donald Grey Barnhouse, for many years an outstanding Bible teacher, has an illustration that goes something like this. He says the Christian and the Lord are distinguishable. He says our Lord Jesus is like the sun. Jesus said, "I am the light of the world." During the day when the sun is shining, it's bright. But when Jesus went back to the Father, it became like night. The church is like the moon; it reflects the Great Light. During times of revival the church is a full moon, reflecting the light of the sun. But other times the church is in carnality and away from its Lord; then it's like a new moon: just a little sliver of light reflecting the light of the Son of God who said, "I am the light of the world."

The Christian only can reflect the light, he cannot shine on his own. Jesus is the light and the reason the world is in darkness is because it only gets reflected light, and we don't always reflect very well. The church ought to be a full moon that reflects the light of Jesus Christ. We don't initiate light, we reflect it; and light comes to bring us into the truth.[1]

However, you can misuse light. Notice verse 15: "Nor do men light a lamp, and put it under the peckmeasure, but on the lampstand; and it gives light to all who are in the house."

Here's the picture: Every little house, those humble little cottages they had in Palestine, had a stone shelf jutting out of an inside wall. On it was a tray filled with oil. Floating on the oil was a wick which was always lit. During the day when they didn't need the light it would be covered over with a little ceramic peckmeasure to keep it from being blown out. If they went away from the home and returned after dark, everyone would stumble around until the little peckmeasure was taken off the light. They couldn't flick a switch or light a match; they didn't have them.

That's the picture Jesus used. He says the church is sometimes like that—with a little peckmeasure over its light. People are stumbling around. We need to lift the cover and let the light be seen. People have need, but the Christian can hide the light so that the world cannot see it.

It can be very embarrassing when you have worked on a job for a long time and some Monday morning one of your co-workers says, "I didn't realize you were a Christian!" He saw you at church on Sunday. Bad news. Nobody knew. You were playing peckmeasure, hiding the light, being so subtle no one ever discovered it. That's a misuse of light. When it doesn't illumine, when it doesn't shine, it is useless.

What is the sphere of your light? "A city set on a hill cannot be hidden." That's a very public witness. The last few years many people whose names are well known have made a very public profession of their faith in Christ. Charles Colson's book, *Born Again,* told the world that he had become a Christian; a football coach from southern Illinois confesses from a hilltop that he is a Christian. Bob Dylan—are you familiar with his story?— came to Christ a while back. Bob Dylan is a Jew who has been through all the mystical religions; then he came to Christ. He was discipled and kept under wraps for a while to protect him from the glare of the public until he was ready with his testimony.

An interesting story concerning Bob Dylan is told by World Vision International. That organization wanted to do something to help the people of Cambodia. They wondered how they could raise the millions of dollars they would need. So they decided to write a letter and have it delivered to Bob Dylan, asking him to do a concert to raise money for Cambodian relief.

They wrote the letter and were trying to figure out who knew Bob Dylan well enough to get it to him when his manager called and said, "Bob would like to do some benefit concerts for World Vision. Is it possible that he could do one for Cambodia?" Of course World Vision was overjoyed. He did four concerts at the Santa Monica Auditorium in California. Tickets went on sale for $15 and $18.50; all four concerts sold out in half a day.

In one of his concerts—not the ones for World Vision—people were complaining because it was so Christian. They asked, "Where's the old Bob Dylan?" Some walked out on his performance. But he decided to stick with his new format and not change. Let the world change; he didn't need to. The second night he began to win his way; by the third night it was really outstanding. Bob Dylan has come to the point in his life as a newborn Christian that he can let his light shine. That's really a public light, set on a hill.

But the Scriptures teach about a more private witness as well. Men light a lamp and put it "on the lampstand; and it gives light to all who are in the house" (Matt. 5:15). This is a witness within the home, the office, the car pool. It's the kind of witness all of us can handle; letting the room around us be lit as we stand for the gospel and the standards of the Christian life— sharing Jesus Christ and His saving power. Is it possible that people work with you, drive with you, study with you, shop with you and have never seen that light?

The Scripture says "Be light; let them see the truth of Jesus Christ reflected in you." Why? "That they may see your good works, and glorify your Father who is in heaven" (Matt. 5:16).

The Challenge to Your Life

You don't have to be a Charles Colson or a Bob Dylan. Christ isn't calling for your life to be like a shopping center grand opening. Not at all. He's calling you to be a little light, a little salt. Light in the room; salt in the meat. That's manageable. It's right where you are—to preserve and to illuminate.

"You are the salt of the earth."

"You are the light of the world."

For Further Study

1. As salt, what is our relationship with the world to be?

2. How have you found it difficult to be "light" in your family of origin?

3. How do you find it challenging to be "light" in your current family (with spouse, children, etc.)?

Note

1. James Montgomery Boice, *The Sermon on the Mount*, (Grand Rapids: Zondervan Publishing Co., 1972), p. 80.

Bibliography

Barclay, William. *The Gospel of Matthew*. Vol. 1 Philadelphia: The Westminster Press, 1958.

Bayly, Joseph. *The Gospel Blimp*. Havertown, Pennsylvania: Windward Press, 1960.

Boice, James Montgomery. *The Sermon on the Mount*. Grand Rapids, Michigan: Zondervan Publishing House, 1972.

Evans, Colleen Townsend. *A New Joy*. Old Tappan, New Jersey: Fleming H. Revell Company, 1973.

Graham, Billy. *The Secret of Happiness!* New York: Pocket Books, 1955.

Lloyd-Jones, D. Martyn. *Studies in the Sermon on the Mount*. Grand Rapids, Michigan: Wm. B. Eerdmans Publishing Company, 1977.

Powell, John, S. J. *Unconditional Love*. Niles, Illinois: Argus Communications, 1978.

Quebedeaux, Richard. *The Worldly Evangelicals*. New York: Harper and Row, Publishers, 1978.

Stott, John R. W. *Christian Counter-Culture*. Downers Grove, Illinois: Inter-Varsity Press, 1978.

Wiersbe, Warren W. *Live Like a King*. Chicago: Moody Press, 1977.